CLARINGTO
COUF

306.8743 Ste

Stewart, G.
Teen mothers.

PRICE: $24.50 (3803/cc)

THE other AMERICA

Teen MOTHERS

by
Gail B. Stewart

Lucent Books, P.O. Box 289011, San Diego, CA 92198-9011

These and other titles are included in *The Other America* series:

    The Elderly
    The Homeless
    People with AIDS

Library of Congress Cataloging-in-Publication Data

Stewart, Gail, 1949-
    Teen mothers / by Gail B. Stewart
      p. cm.—(The other America)
    Includes bibliographical references (p.) and index.
    ISBN 1-56006-332-7 (alk. paper)
    1. Teenage mothers—United States—Interviews—Juvenile literature.
I.Title. II. Series.
HQ759.4.S75   1996
306.874'3—dc20   95-40340
                                                                             CIP
                                                                               AC

The opinions of and stories told by the people in this book are entirely their own. The author has presented their accounts in their own words, and has not verified their accuracy. Thus, the author can make no claim as to the objectivity of their accounts.

No part of this book may be reproduced or used in any form or by any means, electrical, mechanical, or otherwise, including, but not limited to, photocopy, recording, or any information storage and retrieval system, without prior written permission from the publisher.

                        Printed in the U.S.A.
                 Copyright © 1996 by Lucent Books, Inc.
             P.O. Box 289011, San Diego, CA 92198-9011

Contents

FOREWORD	4
INTRODUCTION	6
KAY	10
Pregnant at fifteen, nineteen-year-old Kay's advice to sexually active teenagers is having a child is not fun. Taking care of her little girl is difficult and challenging, especially when Kay would like to experience some of the freedom of being like any other childless young woman.	
SAFA	29
At seventeen, Safa is the mother of a two-year-old son. As a child and young adult, Safa had little direction or love from her drug-addicted mother. Becoming sexually active was a way to feel close and connected to someone.	
LISA	50
Lisa first became sexually active as a freshman in high school and became pregnant that year. Now the mother of a two-year-old son, Lisa is pleased with her child, but leads a difficult life.	
MARY	73
Sexually active at fourteen, pregnant at seventeen, Mary loves being the mother of her baby. Life is difficult, though, as Mary struggles to make the relationship with the baby's father work, live on her own, and take care of Cozette.	
EPILOGUE	91
WAYS YOU CAN GET INVOLVED	92
FOR FURTHER READING	93
INDEX	94
ABOUT THE AUTHOR	96

Foreword

O, YES,
I SAY IT PLAIN,
AMERICA NEVER WAS AMERICA TO ME.
AND YET I SWEAR THIS OATH—
AMERICA WILL BE!
    LANGSTON HUGHES

Perhaps more than any other nation in the world, the United States represents an ideal to many people. The ideal of equality—of opportunity, of legal rights, of protection against discrimination and oppression. To a certain extent, this image has proven accurate. But beneath this ideal lies a less idealistic fact—many segments of our society do not feel included in this vision of America.

They are the outsiders—the homeless, the elderly, people with AIDS, teenage mothers, gang members, prisoners, and countless others. When politicians and the media discuss society's ills, the members of these groups are defined as what's wrong with America; they are the people who need fixing, who need help, or increasingly, who need to take more responsibility. And as these people become society's fix-it problem, they lose all identity as individuals and become part of an anonymous group. In the media and in our minds these groups are identified by condition—a disease, crime, morality, poverty. Their condition becomes their identity, and once this occurs, in the eyes of society, they lose their humanity.

The Other America series reveals the members of these groups as individuals. Through in-depth interviews, each person tells his or her unique story. At times these stories are painful, revealing individuals who are struggling to maintain their integrity, their humanity, their lives, in the face of fear, loss, and economic and spiritual hardship. At other times, their tales are exasperating, demonstrating a litany of poor choices, shortsighted thinking, and self-gratification. Nevertheless, their identities remain distinct, their personalities diverse.

As we listen to the people of *The Other America* series describe their experiences they cease to be stereotypically defined and become tangible, individual. In the process, we may begin to understand more profoundly and think more critically about society's problems. When politicians debate, for example, whether the homeless problem is due to a poor economy or lack of initiative, it will help to read the words of the homeless. Perhaps then we can see the issue more clearly. The family who finds itself temporarily homeless because it has always been one paycheck from poverty is not the same as the mother of six who has been chronically chemically dependent. These people's circumstances are not all of one kind, and perhaps we, after all, are not so very different from them. Before we can act to solve the problems of the Other America, we must be willing to look down their path, to see their faces. And perhaps in doing so, we may find a piece of ourselves as well.

Introduction

MUCH TOO YOUNG

It is a story social workers have heard all too often in the past—and are almost certain to hear hundreds of thousands of times in months and years to come. It is the story of a teenage girl who finds herself pregnant and, for all intents and purposes, alone.

"I didn't think I could get pregnant," says one fourteen-year-old girl. "My boyfriend and I thought we were having sex on days that were safe. But I did. And now he's saying that the baby ain't his, and I know it is. The baby even looks like him. My mom don't want me leaving my son with her, so I can't go back to school no more. I don't got no money until my welfare starts, no boyfriend. God, I'm in sad shape."

A RISING TIDE

There have always been teenagers in the United States that have had babies, but the numbers have increased dramatically in the past few years. It is estimated that more than one million teenage girls will become pregnant in 1995—an average of three thousand per day. The United States has a higher rate of teen pregnancy than any nation in the industrialized world.

The high rate of pregnancy is due to a high rate of sexual activity among American teens. While in 1970 only 29 percent of girls between the ages of 15–19 were sexually active, that proportion has climbed to nearly 75 percent in 1995.

Sociologists say many factors contribute to the rising tide of babies born to American teens, especially those in poor neighborhoods, where one baby in four has a teenager for a mother.

"Lots of kids act smart, talk like they know about sex," says one social worker from Minneapolis. "But when it comes down to knowing how babies are conceived—they're babies themselves.

Even many of the kids who are very sexually active haven't got a clue. They keep these stupid ideas alive, like you can't get pregnant if you have intercourse standing up, or you can't get pregnant the first time you have sex. There are dozens of these ideas, and tens of thousands of babies that are living proof that these ideas are just plain garbage."

There is another reason why teenagers are getting pregnant more than ever before—a reason that may surprise many people. The reason is that many teens—both girls and boys—*want* to have babies. Many girls view a baby as a clear sign that they are adults, and sometimes become pregnant to "prove" to their parents that they are too old to be treated like children. Some see a baby as someone who will provide the unconditional love that they lack from their families. For boys, fathering a child is often a sign of manhood—more attainable in some communities than getting a good job.

The profile of teenage mothers is discouraging. They tend to be girls from low-income families. Most are unmarried, and if they marry their babies' fathers, the marriages are statistically doomed to failure.

Social workers say that most teenage mothers—between 80 and 90 percent—come from dysfunctional families, where mental disorders, chemical abuse, and alcoholism are common. The majority of teens who become pregnant also have sexual abuse in their past—from fathers, stepfathers, or other family members.

A Grim Future

A teen mom's future, like her past, will also be bleak. Physically, the pregnancy and birth will take a toll on her body that is far worse than that suffered by mothers in their twenties and thirties. Because the bones of a teenager are not mature, giving birth will be more difficult.

Teenage girls are less likely to get prenatal care, either because they are embarrassed or ashamed, or because they do not understand how important such care is for them and their unborn babies. The mortality rate for teenage mothers in labor is two and a half times higher than for mothers who are older.

More than 50 percent will drop out of junior high or high school—forty thousand each year in the United States. Few will ever return. Fewer than 5 percent of teens that have babies will make it to college. Not surprisingly, the majority of teenage mothers will follow a downward spiral into poverty and welfare.

THE POLITICS OF TEENAGE MOTHERS

Americans spend a huge amount of money on welfare for teenage mothers—$34 billion each year. Statistically they are the group that is least likely to climb out of the welfare situation. The average stay on welfare for a teenage mother is eight years—longer than any other recipient group.

Such figures have been discouraging, both to government policymakers and taxpayers alike. It is not surprising that politicians have offered suggestions on how to change what all agree is a bad situation.

Early in 1995 President Bill Clinton proposed a plan that would limit the amount of time a teen mother could stay on welfare. He wants to stop a teen mom's benefits after two years—whether or not she has found work. He proposes to make the fathers of babies born to teen mothers pay, too.

According to his plan, mothers would be required to identify the fathers of their babies before they could draw their first welfare check. These fathers would be required to help with the economic support of mother and child, or their driver's licenses would be revoked.

Conservative Newt Gingrich, Speaker of the House of Representatives, has proposed a more drastic plan. He urges that the government deny cash payments and welfare to any new teen mother who is not married. The money saved by his plan, he says, could build orphanages or group homes for teen mothers and their children, where, while teen moms would be cared for, they would not receive cash payment.

GETTING MORE SPECIFIC

Teen moms and their babies have formed a huge social and economic problem for society. While few would disagree that children suffer when they are born outside of a stable, two-parent family, once children are born, what to do becomes society's problem. How can teenagers, who no matter how grown-up they think they are, be made more aware of the fact that bearing children is a serious responsibility? How can teenagers be made to take precautions to prevent pregnancy?

Four teenage mothers are featured in this book. In some ways their situations are very different; in others they are much alike.

Safa is bitter and depressed. Although she loves her two-year-old son, she is pessimistic that she can raise him well—she lives in a high-crime area and has very little income. Kay is also depressed. Her daughter is a daily reminder, she says, "that I am different from other girls my age, and I don't like it."

Mary enjoys being a mother, but is unsure of what her boyfriend's role in their lives will be. "We're giving it six months to see," she says, "and we'll go on from there."

Lisa enjoys watching her young son grow. It is not something she planned, she says, but she is not discouraged or depressed. "I wouldn't do it again," she says, "but I'm not going to let having a baby stop me from doing the stuff I want to do."

Some of these stories are disturbing—more than one of these girls have endured childhoods of unspeakable violence. Their stories reveal both admirable qualities and extreme immaturity and self-centeredness. Many show how vulnerable both the mothers and their babies are, and how tentative their futures. All give a bird's-eye view into four lives of the Other America.

Kay

> "I WAS SO SURPRISED—I DIDN'T HAVE A CLUE AT ALL THAT I COULD BE PREGNANT. . . . I HAD BEEN ON BIRTH CONTROL, BUT . . . I REMEMBERED THAT I'D MISSED A FEW DAYS."

If any young teenager is thinking about getting pregnant, or is even thinking about having sex, Kay has advice for her: don't. Don't do anything unless you can be 100 percent sure that you aren't going to wind up pregnant.

Kay is a pretty nineteen-year-old who feels, quite frankly, as though her life stopped when she learned she was pregnant at age fifteen. And until that teenage life was cut short, Kay says, she never really knew how precious it was.

"I look at girls today who are talking about having babies," she says. "I hear them sometimes, really excited about being pregnant. I just shake my head and think, 'Have fun.' I mean, I really do hope they enjoy it more than I have. I just look at my own daughter and pray that she never has to go through what I'm going through. I want her to have the life that I know I'm never going to have."

From South America to North Dakota

Kay's life started in South America, where she was adopted by a couple from North Dakota when she was just a few months old.

"My own mother gave me up. I'm not sure why," she says. "My adoptive parents came to Colombia to pick up two kids that they'd already picked out. That's the rule—at least it was the rule back then—that you have to go to Colombia to get the child you're adopting. The kids don't just come on the plane to the United States the way they do from some countries.

"Anyway, they got there, and the children they'd planned to adopt had died. They got me instead, and another Colombian baby who became sort of an instant brother for me."

Her new family was large; with the addition of the two Colombian infants, there were nine children. They lived on a farm at first, but when Kay was about four, the family moved to Minneapolis.

"It seems really brave, when you think about it," Kay says thoughtfully. "My father didn't have any job or anything lined up in the city. He and my mom wanted to move because they felt we'd get a better education here. The farm was nice, but they said the schools just weren't as good.

"My mom had always been a housewife, but when they moved she took in some kids for day care, just to help out with the finances. My dad got a job at Reach Out—that's a thrift store. Later on he got a job as a realtor, so things worked out."

Mixed Memories

Kay has pleasant memories of growing up in the big house in the city. The family lived on a pleasant, tree-lined street, and there were lots of children her age to play with.

"We had toys and everything, but mostly we played with each other," she remembers with a smile. "I mean, there were nine of us kids, just in our family alone! And there were kids all over, all around the block and across the street, that we could do things with. When I think of summer, I think of playing Ships Across the Ocean, or tag, or having a Kool-Aid stand on the corner. There were always things to do."

But there were other parts of her childhood that she tries not to remember, or if she does remember them, it is with anger and revulsion.

"I was raped as a child—repeatedly," she says softly. "My grandpa did it to me. He lived in North Dakota still, and when we would go back to the farm for visits, he would rape me.

"My mother didn't know it was going on until much later, when I eventually told her what happened. But she never guessed before that. When I told her about it, I learned that he had done the same thing to my aunts when they were younger. The whole thing is really hard for me to think about, and it's even harder to talk about. It was a really bad part of my life, one that I'd rather just forget. I'd rather concentrate on the happier times in the city."

Kay has heard the statistics—that a majority of teens who become pregnant were the victims of sexual abuse as children—and they don't surprise her.

"I did become sexually active early," she admits. "I mean, the father of my child wasn't the first boy I had a relationship with. But I look back on it now, and I think that being raped like that had a lot to do with me starting sex earlier than lots of girls. I'm

Kay's introduction to sex was brutal: "I was raped as a child—repeatedly. . . . I think that being raped like that had a lot to do with me starting sex earlier than lots of girls."

not really using it as an excuse or anything, but I'm sure being abused like that made a difference in my life. It's like I skipped other stuff that kids did and went right to that grown-up part, or something."

Kay shakes her head.

"I don't know, it's hard to explain."

"I Didn't Have a Clue at All"

"I was a freshman in high school when I got pregnant. I was pretty happy at school—I liked it. My parents were divorced by then, but I was handling it okay. I stayed close to my father. We went out to eat and talked a lot. He was always really interested to hear what I was doing, how things were going with my friends at school.

"Really, high school was a lot more fun than grade school had been. The kids were different, I think. I mean, back in the Catholic grade schools I'd gone to, I was always in the popular clique, but it was a lot of pressure. You didn't want to make the leaders of the clique mad, because if they were mad at you, they'd talk behind your back, and everyone would hate you. But once I got to high school, it was better. I was still in the popular clique, but we had friends in all the groups. We talked to everybody.

"Anyway, I was pretty active at school, like I said. I was athletic, so I was on the soccer team and dance line. That was how I found out about being pregnant, in fact. I had to have a physical once I made dance line during my freshman year—that was the rule. Before any girls could participate, they had to have the forms filled out."

Because her family did not have medical insurance, Kay was given a physical examination at school. It was then that she received the news.

"I was told to wait outside," she remembers. "I was just sitting out in the hall, sitting on a bench. Then the nurse came out and told me they had some news for me. I went back in the office and she told me I was pregnant.

"I was so surprised—I didn't have a clue at all that I could be pregnant. I couldn't believe it. I guess I was just speechless for a few minutes. I had been on birth control, but when I thought back, I remembered that I'd missed a few days. That was what did it, I guess."

Dealing with It

Kay knew right away who the father of her baby was—a boy named Tony to whom she'd been introduced at a party.

"He was older than me, about twenty," says Kay. "Some of my high school friends had known him and liked him right away. We were kind of going out for a while. Then, about two months later, I was pregnant."

Her first reaction, other than shock, was just to leave, Kay remembers.

"That physical was during lunch hour," she says. "There was no way I could go back to English class or whatever. I just took off. Later that night I told my girlfriends. I was really careful about who to tell, because news like that travels fast, believe me. So I told people I could trust.

"I told Tony. He was absolutely no help. His reaction was, 'So what are you going to do?' Not anything about 'we' or 'us' mak-

Tony's reaction to Kay's pregnancy was rather typical: "So what are you going to do?" While it takes two to make a baby, the responsibility for the child typically becomes the young, unwed, teenage mother's.

ing a decision. So I knew I wasn't going to get any support from the baby's father."

Kay *did* go to her mother, but it was not to tell her about the pregnancy. Interestingly, it was to reveal the news of her being raped as a child.

"I just couldn't tell her yet," says Kay, a little embarrassed. "I didn't let her know I was pregnant until a few months later, when I was five months along. I just thought I better tell her about the rape first, let her think about that. She was sad for me and probably felt guilty, I don't really know."

THE ABORTION ATTEMPT

Kay had no strong feelings against abortion. In this case it seemed the best way to correct a mistake, she says. With this in mind, she and a couple of close friends planned a trip to an abortion clinic north of the city.

"It was my friends Laura and Lindsey that planned the whole thing out," she says. "Laura and I slept over at Lindsey's. The next day we left about 5:00 A.M. on the bus. It was a really long ride, with transfers. None of us really knew how to get there, so it was kind of stressful. They were trying to be really loyal, but all I felt was nervousness. I didn't want to think too much about what I was doing, you know?

"My friends had helped by loaning me money. I had a job working at Godfather's Pizza, but I sure didn't make enough for the abortion. Anyway, when we got to the clinic, I found out I was late. I mean, not late for my appointment, but late in my pregnancy. I was three months along, and that changed everything. The clinic could still do the abortion, but it would be more complicated, and way more expensive.

"I guess I had an option. I could have made another appointment and come back again. But all I wanted, if you want to know the truth, was to just go home and go to bed. I was crying and stressed out and nervous. I just wanted to go home to my own room and cry. I knew I couldn't go back to that place."

"I JUST HATED THEM"

"I finally decided, after that whole episode at the abortion clinic, that I would keep the baby," says Kay. "And I also knew I better let my family know about it before I started to show."

Her mother was shocked, Kay remembers. She was adamant that Kay could not abort the baby; she insisted that Kay either keep it or put it up for adoption.

"I understand why my mom felt that way," says Kay. "I mean, she raised all of us kids Catholic and everything. She didn't believe in abortion as an option to an unwanted pregnancy. But she was also pretty angry about it. She didn't even know I was on birth control or anything, so it was a real shock for her.

"My dad was the real surprise. I was dreading telling him. We had always been so close. He didn't know I was sexually active, either. I felt like I was letting him down. I was afraid to face him, but I really thought that he'd be supportive of me.

"I was wrong. I told him in the car, when we were coming

Kay expected more help from her parents: "Boy, lots of girls in my situation have parents that would let their daughter live with them. . . . My parents [told] me that once the baby's born, I'm out on my own."

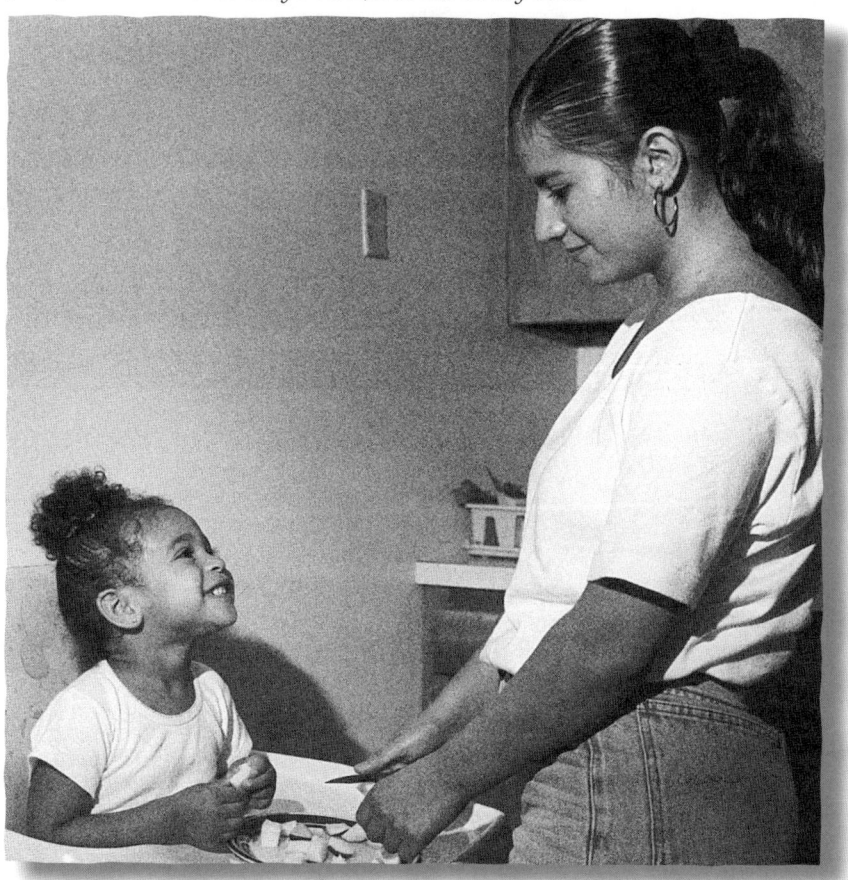

16

home from dinner one night. He was so mad—it was like I was really on my own. He said, 'Boy, Kay, you did this and you're going to suffer for it.' That was really hard on me."

Kay admits that she was as angry with her parents as they were with her, especially in those first months.

"I kept thinking to myself, boy, lots of girls in my situation have parents that would let their daughter live with them, and they'd take care of the baby when the daughter is in school or out with her friends, or whatever. And here my parents are telling me that once the baby's born, I'm out on my own. I mean, I was just turning fifteen, a freshman in high school, and I was going to be on my own with a little baby. I was so mad at them, I can't even describe it. I just hated them, I really did."

"SHE'S THE ONLY FAMILY I HAVE"

Kay is interrupted by a high-pitched voice calling, "Mama, I brush my teeth. I brush my teeth."

Kay giggles.

"She's really into brushing her teeth now. I wish she was as interested in using her potty chair!"

Jasmine runs into the room, breathless. She smiles shyly at her mother's guests and runs headlong into Kay's arms.

"Slow down, Jas," Kay admonishes.

"She has so much energy," Kay sighs, "that it's hard to keep up with her."

Jasmine moves around her mother on the couch, trying to lie in Kay's lap, needing attention. Every few minutes she coughs—a croupy-sounding bark.

"I don't know what's with that cough," says Kay. "Anyway, I was pretty much on my own after I told my parents about being pregnant. And since I didn't really want to go through with an abortion, I was stuck."

Was adoption ever an alternative?

Kay shakes her head.

"It was an alternative for my mom," Kay says, absentmindedly stroking Jasmine's hair. "I mean, she was dead set against abortion, but adoption was something she suggested. But not me. I couldn't do that. I wouldn't even consider it. I couldn't abandon her like that. Once I made the decision not to have the abortion, I was deciding to keep that baby, you know?

"I mean, I was adopted. I should know that it's okay to give a baby up. But I just couldn't do it. She's the only family I have, the only flesh and blood that's like me. I couldn't get rid of her on someone else."

HAVING THE BABY

Kay says that she changed schools when her pregnancy started to show, and that was a little bit of a relief.

"It was more comfortable going to the alternative school for teenage moms," she explains. "Nobody was judging you, you know? But there was a lot of talking, a lot of gossiping about who was going with who, who is who's baby's father, like that. I hate gossip; I really hate the talking. But as far as the parenting classes, the education, the relief to be pregnant and not feel like a freak, that was much better."

Even so, she dropped out of school toward the end of her pregnancy. "It was too hard to do the work," she says. "Besides that, it was really hard to get up every morning. I was always so tired."

Jasmine's birth began on Christmas Eve, on a very cold night. Kay's memories of going to the hospital are not pleasant ones.

"It was the county hospital downtown, and it was confusing to get into. It was a really cold night, and we couldn't find the right entrance to the hospital, so we ended up walking around the whole stupid parking lot. The wind was blowing, it was really slippery and icy.

"And that hospital was the worst hospital in the whole world," she says with disgust. "I mean it. All these bums all over the place—it just wasn't where I wanted to have a baby. And just when we walked in, there was this guy just going crazy, yelling and screaming. I don't know if he was on drugs or just insane. But I was scared already, and that really made me come apart, you know?

"It was not a terrible birth or anything. Nothing I couldn't manage. My mom and my one sister were there with me, so that was good. But I had this big disappointment. It seems so stupid, but it meant a lot to me. The baby was born on Christmas Day, and usually the newspaper has a photographer come and take a picture of babies born on Christmas, has them in Christmas stockings, you know? I think it's a really cute thing that they do, but Jasmine didn't get her picture taken like that. I was so mad."

Kay felt pretty isolated after the birth of her daughter: "She was a pretty little baby, but I really didn't have much feeling for her one way or another. . . . When she was first born, I said to my mom, 'I don't even love her.'"

"IT DIDN'T SEEM RIGHT NOT TO LOVE HER"

The first hours after the birth of her baby went by in a flurry for Kay, who says she was so tired that she was unaware of what was going on.

The baby's father, Tony, was present at the birth. "When I woke up from the medicine they'd given me, the baby already had a name," she says. "Tony had named her Jasmine, and his mother had given her the middle name of Noel, since it was Christmas. That was okay; I didn't really mind that they did that. I hadn't thought that much about names beforehand, and Jasmine is as good as any name. I mean, that way I didn't have to worry about choosing one in the hospital. They did it all for me.

"But," Kay says, "I remember being really mad, because they had decided her last name would be Tony's, not mine. That seemed wrong, and it still seems wrong now. The way things are, with Tony not being a part of her life at all, why should she have his name and not mine? The whole decision was made when I was sleeping, after she was born. It was weird."

Kay remembers that it felt strange not to have strong emotions toward her newborn daughter.

"She was a pretty little baby, but I really didn't have much feeling for her one way or another. I admit it. When she was first born, I said to my mom, 'I don't even love her.' She told me not to worry, that everyone feels that way when they first have a baby. I don't know if she was saying that to make me feel better, or what. I cried, because it didn't seem right not to love her, you know? I wasn't excited, or happy, or anything. It just seemed like a lot of work."

Kay says that at the time of the birth, she and Tony were trying to get along, hoping that maybe Jasmine would provide a bond in their relationship that wasn't there before.

"He stuck by me for a while, I guess," she says. "For a while, when the baby was real small we had an apartment together. But it didn't work out. It was dumb that we even tried, I think. He cheated on me a lot, that much I know for sure.

"And he wasn't interested in the baby, either. She'd cry, and he'd say to me, 'Go get her.' I don't think he cared one bit."

ON MY OWN

The arrangement with Tony fell apart soon afterwards.

"He called one day and asked me what the code for our answering machine was—you know, the one you use to retrieve your messages? I'm not sure why he couldn't remember it. Anyway, I was just kidding around and I told him I wouldn't tell him, or I would tell him later, or something.

"Anyway, later he came home from work and brought all his friends. They all grabbed furniture and started moving everything out of the apartment. I mean, they were taking everything—tables, the bed, the television, everything.

"I called my mom. I didn't know what to do. My mom's boyfriend came over and told me to come home to my mom's house, that if I stayed where I was, it would make me too upset. I just couldn't believe Tony could pull something like that. He left me a dresser and a bassinet. That's all—plus the baby, of course. I still think of that as being one of the worst days of my life. I just felt so helpless, watching those guys moving away all that stuff."

Money was tight. Kay was receiving a welfare check for $437 each month, which was the amount of her rent. She knew she couldn't afford the place on her own.

"I kept saying to myself, not only can't I afford this place, I don't want to live by myself," she says. "It was too scary. I was used to having lots of brothers and sisters around, lots of noise and stuff going on. The idea of being in this quiet apartment all alone with a baby just freaked me out.

"So I started calling all the people I knew, saying, 'Do you want to come live with me?' I finally got hold of this girl I'd met. She was a few years older but had a boyfriend and a baby. They had a one-room apartment smaller than my living room now. And so I left my apartment and went to live with them."

The experience, says Kay, was a disaster.

"It was miserable," she says, shuddering at the memory. "Five of us living in this grimy, dirty place. It was worse than being alone. There were people tramping in and out all the time, because we had lots of friends. They had no furniture either; they were worse off than I was. My dad bought me a futon, and we all took turns, alternating on who got to sleep on it.

"I had a little baby; I was getting up in the middle of the night to feed her. The place was either too hot or too cold, and both babies were sick all the time. We were there for a few months, and then we got evicted."

"The Whole Thing Was Like a Baby-Sitting Job for Me"

Kay says that her lack of strong emotion toward Jasmine continued and that she often felt like an outsider as Tony's family fussed over the baby.

"I don't want to say anything bad about Tony's mom," Kay insists. "She's been really good. She loves babies. I mean, Jasmine calls her Nana, and is really close to her. I think that Tony's mom was more into Jasmine than I was, to tell you the truth."

Why was that? Kay squints, trying to verbalize her thoughts.

"I think there were a couple of reasons," she says. "For one thing, I really wanted to keep an arm's length from that family. I didn't want to join in with what Tony's mom was doing, because of my strange relationship with Tony and all.

"But there was that other thing. I just didn't bond, or whatever you call it, with Jasmine right away. Tony's mom helped; she bought things so the baby had stuff. But I didn't really want to get into it. I didn't feel like I was part of the whole thing. I felt like I

Tony's mother devotes a lot of time and energy to Jasmine. Kay has mixed feelings about her involvement: "I think that Tony's mom was more into Jasmine than I was, to tell you the truth."

was watching, you know? But not really *doing* anything. I was Jasmine's mom, but I really didn't feel like it.

"The whole thing was like a baby-sitting job for me at first. I'd take care of her, but no emotional feelings, that's for sure. But there was Tony's mom, saying, 'If you don't want her, I'll take her.' Stuff like that. It made me feel even stranger than I already felt. You know what I mean?"

AMBIGUITY

Even though Tony's leaving hurt her, Kay says that she had second thoughts about ending their relationship soon afterwards.

"It's hard to explain," she says with a nervous giggle. "After he moved out, after a few weeks I started talking to him again. He was my baby's dad, after all. I kind of went through some thinking then—should I go back with him or should I just be on my own?

"But then, I thought, hey, he's Jasmine's father. Every parent should see their baby whenever they want, I think. So I let him see her when he wanted to. He could take her whenever he wanted. It was no big deal to me."

Kay says that during this time she became involved with another young man whom she'd known all through high school.

"It was strange," she says, "because Tony's calling me, saying that he still loved me and did I want to marry him. And then I was seeing Tano. He's the guy I'm with a lot now. Tano is really nice; I really love him a lot. And he's changed a lot toward Jasmine, too.

"Before, in high school, I just talked to Tano. We were friends. And when I started seeing him recently, he acted kind of strange toward Jasmine. He didn't want anything to do with her. I think he was scared. I'd say, 'Will you watch her while I run into the bathroom?' and he'd be saying, 'That's not my baby. I'm not responsible.' That kind of thing. I don't know, maybe Tano was jealous of Tony.

"But anyway, Tano is really better about her now. He's come a long way since he didn't want to watch her even for a minute. He watches her when I'm at work—no problem. He buys her clothes, gets her a Popsicle when we're out somewhere, stuff like that. He takes over the part that Tony should be doing. I think Jasmine considers Tano as more her daddy than Tony."

What about Tony's role in Jasmine's life? Kay snorts and rolls her eyes.

"He doesn't really have one," Kay says. "I might have been tempted at one time to go back with Tony, but I know now I'll never do that. I hated the situation I was in, and I hated him for putting me there, you know?

"Anyway, I see Tano now. It's nothing permanent. I don't ever want to get married. I don't mind when Tano wants to go out with his friends. It doesn't bother me at all. I know some girls get all crazy when their boyfriends aren't going out with them all the time, but I'm not like that. I have no intention of getting serious about anyone, so there's no pressure on him."

"I Wish I Could Go Out Drinking Every Night"

Kay is not happy with the way her life is going, but there is very little she can do to change things, she says. Although she lives in her own apartment, financially she is struggling, even with help.

"I get money from Project Solo. That's a government program that helps me pay my rent. I get welfare money for Jasmine and food stamps. My dad gives me three hundred dollars each month to help out. That's great, but I don't feel that I have enough. I used to have a part-time job at a cleaner's, but now that I'm going to school, I don't work there. I miss the extra money, though, that's for sure."

She finds herself becoming jealous of the way other girls with babies are living, including many of the girls with whom she attends school.

"It seems like a lot of the girls are better equipped for this than I am. Lots of them grow up helping their moms take care of babies, their sisters had babies early, or something like that. They know how to do most of this stuff, especially the black girls at my school. Most of my friends at the school I went to—the one for teenage moms—were black, so I think I can say that.

"Some of these girls . . . I'm serious, they were twelve, thirteen, and fourteen years old, and had two or three kids! I mean, I feel sorry for myself, but when I see them, I'm like, my goodness!

"But they get lots of help, usually. Their moms or their grandmas raise the kids; the girls just keep doing what they've always done. But not me. I know I have Tony's mom, and that's fine. She takes Jasmine places, and Jasmine really loves her.

"My mom isn't as active with Jasmine as Tony's mom is. I think she'll be better when Jasmine's older. But my mom has been a mother for so long, raising so many kids, I think she's tired. She still has a daughter who's thirteen, so I think my mom doesn't have the time to be a full-time grandma, you know? She's raised nine kids; that's a lot. She's been a mother since she was seventeen, and she's over fifty, now."

Instead, says Kay, she herself is the one who has to be dependable.

"And I hate being dependable!" she says with a bitter laugh. "Like, I know girls who get high in front of their kids or get drunk. But I don't. Hey, I wish I could go out drinking every night and sleep in until one o'clock the next afternoon. That's the life I wish I had. I'm so mad that everything turned out this way. I get jealous of other people, of how they live, the things they do. I hear girls say, 'I'm going to go to college in Florida.' I wish I could go to college in Florida. I want to go to a college far away, someplace great like Florida."

"I'VE GOT NO SOCIAL LIFE"

But for now, Kay says, that kind of life is very remote. Her social life is quite dull, in fact, compared to that of most girls her age.

"I have school," she says in a bored voice. "I'm taking history and some other courses I need to graduate and be done. I don't mind science classes; those are okay. I think I'd like to be a nurse someday. But I hate reading. When people talk about curling up with a good book, I can't even imagine it. I never could.

The restrictions of motherhood are not a pleasure for Kay: "I hate being dependable! . . . I know girls who get high in front of their kids or get drunk. But I don't."

"What I *would* like to do is to go to a party or hang out with my friends—do stuff with people my own age. Shopping is fun, too. I enjoy shopping for Jasmine or my apartment. But usually I'm home with Jasmine.

"Really, when you think about it, I've got no social life at all," she says. "I do everything with her. I have a friend from school, Nicole. She has a baby and a boyfriend, and they're good about including me and Jasmine in stuff they do. We go to the park so that the babies can swim in the little pool there. Or we go to their friends' apartment and barbecue.

"When Jasmine and I are on our own, we go to the park. We play ball or just walk around. She swings. She's really into getting dressed; she has opinions on what she wants to wear all of a sudden. She's got really pretty hair, and it's fun for us to put it in different styles. Jasmine gets mad if there are tangles, though, so I have to be quick about it."

Kay picks up a cracker from the floor.

"Jasmine will be happier when I get a car. Both of us will. She gets bored in here, always asks if we can go somewhere. We've been stuck without a car for a while, ever since mine broke down. The new one I'm getting is in the shop, but it shouldn't be too much longer. I hope."

THEY THINK HE CARES, BUT HE DOESN'T

Kay admits she is in a somewhat negative mood today, for she has just had a fight with Tony's sister, Amber. Amber and Kay often lock horns, she says, because they see two different sides of Tony.

"She's really opinionated, really outspoken for a fifteen-year-old," says Kay. "It really bothers me, too. She talks to me all the time about Tony, about how great he is, what a great father. Things she doesn't know, she acts like she does.

"I don't think I'm a grown-up person or anything, but I still don't think a fifteen-year-old should be talking to a nineteen-year-old that way. I don't know how she gets away with it, but she does.

"The fight we just had had to do with Father's Day, just last week. I didn't give him a present or have Jasmine give one to Tony. Amber says, 'You could at least have given him a card.' She told me about how Tony gave me a card on Mother's Day."

Kay scoffs.

"Yeah, right. Tony's mother bought it, I'm sure. Tony would never think to do something like that. His family thinks he cares, but he doesn't. Anyway, no matter who bought it, it meant nothing to me. When Jasmine's older and she goes out and does something on her own, buys a gift or a card or flowers or something, that will be a different story. But please, don't tell me how much I should appreciate Tony's mom giving me a card that supposedly was from Tony!

"I don't care about Tony at all. I know I've been talking a lot about him, but I really don't care. He lives with his parents, in their basement, and he goes in and out. He'll stop if Jasmine's over there and say hi to her, but it's not like he's really *with* her, you know? He just says 'Hi' and keeps right on going. He'll see her by accident, only because his mom is watching her."

"I'll give you an example of how little he cares. The other day I called to see if he could watch Jasmine for two hours. He works as

Kay is frustrated by what she sees as Tony's lack of involvement: "The other day I called to see if he could watch Jasmine for two hours. . . . But he said no, . . . he had to work on his friend's car."

27

a dealer at the casino, and I knew he didn't have to be at work until six o'clock, but it was three o'clock then, so I thought he would. But he said no, like he usually does. No, he had to work on his friend's car."

Kay shrugs. "I can talk to him a little, but that's it. He lost out, missed out on his chance to be a part of Jasmine's life. So when Amber gives me a big lecture about not giving Tony a card for Father's Day, I think, what for? He never buys things, never even acts interested. A father figure is not that important. Better not to have one than to have one like Tony."

She shakes her head.

"So, fine. When I need someone to watch Jasmine, it's my problem. You know what? It usually is."

"Every Day It Goes Through My Head"

Kay says that the one thing being a teenage mother has taught her is to be protective of Jasmine.

"I'm going to be really watching out for her when she's fourteen, fifteen," says Kay emphatically. "I want to be open with her; I don't want her to be afraid to tell me things she's thinking about or things she's doing. I want her to be open with me. I'm going to make sure she never goes out with a twenty-year-old guy when she's a freshman in high school, I'll tell you that much."

When was the first time she looked at Jasmine and was glad? Kay's eyes fill with tears, and she self-consciously wipes them away. She takes a long time formulating an answer.

"I like it when I dress her up and we go to a family thing. It's fun when everybody makes a big deal fussing over her, saying she's so cute. That's nice."

Kay pauses again.

"And I like making her happy. It's fun to see her when I tell her we're going somewhere or when I buy her a present that she really likes. But other than that, I'm not glad she's born. Mostly, I'm sad.

"Every day it goes through my head; I can't stop thinking about it. I feel guilty, too, like I'm supposed to think a different way. I just live with it, though. I mean, maybe someday I'll get to a point where I'm glad she's here. I hope so. I can't imagine being like this for her whole life. I don't know what I'd do."

Safa

> "I [HAD SEX] BECAUSE THE BOYS WANTED TO. . . . IT MADE ME FEEL LIKE THEY REALLY LOVED ME."

His name is Mahari, and he is a two-year-old bundle of energy. In fact, his mother, Safa, admits, he can be a real terror when he wants to be. This afternoon Safa and Mahari are sitting on the floor of his room, putting pennies into a bank the shape of a crayon.

"What he does is wait until all these pennies are picked up," explains Safa, "and then the minute I walk away, he spills the bank and they're all on the floor again. I don't know why—if it's the noise they make or just seeing me get mad. But he loves to do it, that's for sure.

"Today it's the pennies," she says, looking around the room strewn with toys. "Yesterday it was the VCR. It doesn't work anymore, so he can't watch his tapes."

She looks at her son accusingly.

"Hey, Mahari, why doesn't your VCR work?"

Mahari's smile fades, and he suddenly takes an interest in the penny in the palm of his hand.

"The VCR doesn't work," Safa explains, "because yesterday he stuck a slice of cheese in it. That's why."

"I Don't Really Feel Like I'm Seventeen"

Safa is a strikingly pretty young woman, with large, heavily lidded eyes and a model's smile. She is seventeen, although she talks like someone years older.

At seventeen, Safa has to struggle to keep up with her active son and maintain a household: "I really love Mahari and everything, but it's a scary thing, being a mother, living the way I do."

"I have a son, have an apartment I signed the lease for, I go to school, I've had a job," she says with a shrug. "I'm on my own, you know? I don't really feel like I'm seventeen—at least not the same kind of seventeen lots of my friends are.

"I choose not to live at home, and I'm glad of that. So I've got my independence. But it's a hard life; I get so scared sometimes. I sometimes think about what I'm doing, and I wonder if it's the right thing for us. I really love Mahari and everything, but it's a scary thing, being a mother, living the way I do."

Safa says that one of the big reasons she is so uncertain as a mother is her own stormy childhood. It is not a time she remembers with feelings of nostalgia. Quite the contrary, she says; thinking about her upbringing usually leaves her angry and frustrated.

"I Felt Really Cut Off from Other People"

Safa is of mixed race: her mother is Mexican, her father is black. One of five sisters, Safa says that she was very young when her parents divorced.

"Their marriage probably didn't even have a chance," she says, shaking her head. "My mother was so much younger than my dad; she was only sixteen when they got married. Plus, he was a Muslim and she was a Catholic. That was a real hard mix, too.

"My dad was a real strict man, really cold, when I was young," she remembers. "He never ever told me that he loved me—not in my whole life. That's hard to believe, right? He was always the kind of father that if you do something, he's right there telling you, 'You can do much better than that.' He was always hard to please. I couldn't make him proud of me, no matter what I did, no matter how well I did something."

Safa and her sisters were raised Muslim; her name is an Islamic word meaning "purity and happiness." And although their religious upbringing gave their lives structure, she remembers her early years as being very isolated.

"He was really protective and not in a way that made me feel safe," she says. "I felt really cut off from other people. I think that's his religion—the Muslim thing. He was so into living a Muslim life, keeping our family disciplined and everything, he didn't ever want us to be around outsiders. Or if they were outsiders, they had to be Muslim, too. I just remember always being in the house, never playing at other kids' houses, never having a friend."

MY MOM HAS SO MANY PROBLEMS

While her father might have seemed cold and unfeeling toward her, Safa says that most of her problems growing up were the result of conflicts between herself and her mother.

"My mom and I have always had trouble getting along," says Safa, "and most of it has to do with her drinking, her taking drugs. She's had a lot of problems in her life, I know that. I mean, she was raped by her grandfather back in Mexico, and her mother was a prostitute. There was a lot of incest in that family, even with my grandma and my mom's brothers. It's bad, it's hard to talk about.

"So she's had trouble like that since she was little, things in her life that were terrible. Maybe that's why she married my dad, you know? Even though it didn't look like a great marriage, at least it got her out of Mexico and that family.

"Anyway, my mom's had alcohol problems ever since the divorce. At least that's when she got into it pretty heavy. I think she thought that drinking was going to make her feel better or just help her forget about how bad her life was, or something. But anyway, all she did was drink, and I never noticed her feeling any better."

Instead, Safa says, her mother became more and more withdrawn from the family, splitting her time between work and drinking at home.

"Work and drink, that's all she'd do," she says. "She'd come home, wouldn't say much of anything to anybody, and then she'd go off in another room and drink. I have real vivid memories of trying to be around her, even though she wasn't paying me any mind. I just wanted to be underfoot. I was real little, so I think I really needed the attention, you know?"

Safa's childhood was spent with an alcoholic and neglectful mother: "Work and drink, that's all she'd do."

With their mother unable to care for the family, Safa's older sisters took a hand in raising the younger ones. As one of the younger ones, Safa says, she was used to her sisters' telling her what to do.

"That's who raised me," Safa insists, "my older sisters. I probably wasn't crazy about them bossing us around, but I was used to it. And since I was used to my sisters, it wasn't so easy to listen to my mom much when she decided to have some authority. I feel like, she turned us over to our older sisters way back, you know?"

"Our Family Just Came Apart"

Life became decidedly worse for the family when Safa's mother turned from alcohol to crack cocaine. Safa says that it was especially difficult because her mother would deny that she was using the drug. "I don't know when she started exactly," says Safa. "But it was really bad when I was twelve and thirteen—really bad. Our family just came apart. I mean, I *knew* she was on drugs. Hey, lots of my friends from school had mothers on drugs. It's not hard to pick up on, you know? But she denied it. And for some reason, my sisters didn't see it; I don't know why. And when I tried to talk to my mom, to ask her why she was using drugs, she'd get mad, tell me I didn't know what I was talking about.

"A lot of it was this boyfriend she had—Frank. He was the one who got her started, I think. Once my boyfriend told me he'd seen Frank coming out of a crack house, and I asked my mom about that—how come Frank was hanging around some place like that. She just said that Frank would never do nothing like that. Yeah, right."

The constant need to buy more crack depleted the family's budget, a budget that was already strained.

"We all had jobs, even when we were young," Safa says. "We all helped out, but it wasn't enough. My mom and her boyfriend had had good jobs, but they lost their jobs, lost the car, bill collectors hassling us all the time, the phone and lights being turned off. All that because of the drugs.

"I had a summer job, working day care at the Y. The idea was that it was some spending money for me, so I could buy clothes or things I needed.

"But my mom would ask for my check every time I got paid. I'd never see it. A child-support check would come, and we'd ask her for money for shampoo or tampons or something like that, and she'd just play us off, you know, like she didn't hear us."

A Discipline Problem

By the time she was thirteen, Safa's relationship with her mother was at a breaking point.

"It was like I was the only one in the family that was mad at what she was doing to us," Safa says. "I admit sometimes I lose my temper, and I say what's on my mind. But it made me so mad that she wouldn't even try to get help getting off the crack. And she didn't act interested in us one bit; it was like she wasn't there at all. So we had troubles, my mom and me."

Safa says that when she was thirteen, she was sent away from the family to a juvenile home for troubled children.

"My mom called the police and told them to take me to Saint Joe's," she says. "She'd get mad at me because I wasn't coming home at a certain time—and she'd never given me a curfew."

Safa laughs bitterly.

"It was like she had a split personality or something. I mean, she didn't care enough even to know where I was, and then she'd get mad because I wasn't home. It made no sense. So I'd argue with her, and we'd get into these big fights. She'd start snapping on me and hit me, then she'd call the police because I was a discipline problem."

Safa says that she was rarely at home that year. Several times she was at St. Joseph's; other times she stayed with friends from school.

"Sometimes I stayed with boyfriends," she says. "That's the age I was when I started having sexual relationships—thirteen. I can honestly say that I didn't enjoy it. I still don't see what the big thing is about it. I did it because the boys wanted to, you know. It made me feel like they really loved me. I know now that that was wrong, that it was just low self-esteem on my part. But that's how I was at thirteen."

Getting Pregnant

Safa became pregnant when she was in eighth grade, at the age of fourteen.

"His name is Terry," Safa says with no hint of emotion. "I've known him since fourth grade. He's the cousin of my best friend,

Jay, so I'd seen him over at her house on and off almost all my life.

"I actually met him in the hospital; he'd gotten shot in some gang-related stuff," she shrugs. "Trying to prove he's some big man, you know. Anyway, I went along with Jay and her family to see him there, and he really got to me. He was telling me how pretty I was, how he wants me to be his girlfriend. It sounds really silly now, really stupid that I fell for that. But I was fourteen and he was eighteen, and he did a number on me."

Safa admits she should have known she was in for trouble, since Terry had two other children by other girls.

"And," she adds, rolling her eyes, "he's had two other kids since my son was born. So what does that tell you, right? But he was charming, and like I said, he did a number on me."

Safa says she knew she should have been more careful about having sex, since she was not using any birth control.

"Let me rephrase that," she says. "I *had been* on the pill, but my mom found my pills, and she went crazy. She was yelling at me and telling me what a bad girl I was. I was lying to her, telling her I wasn't having sex. She got so mad at me she threw them away, and I never went back in to get more."

"WHAT ARE YOU GOING TO DO?"

Safa had a feeling she might be pregnant, for she was feeling a little sick in the mornings. At first, however, she pushed the thought to the back of her mind.

"My periods were pretty regular—every thirty-one days," she explains. "My friend Jay and I usually had ours at the same time, you know? Anyway, Jay had been in Gary, Indiana, visiting friends. She had just gotten back, and we were having so much fun talking and stuff, and I was so happy to see her again, when all of a sudden she said something about her period. I thought, she's already had hers, why haven't I gotten mine?

"Well, I started really feeling sick then. I figured I must be about eleven days late. I didn't know what I should do. I went in for a pregnancy test and it came back positive. I really thought it would. But I made them do it again. I guess I just didn't want to face it yet, you know?

"I was staying at Jay's house. That was during the time when my mom and I were really fighting all the time about her drugs and her boyfriend. It was fine with Jay and her mom. I mean, Jay is so lucky. She's got the nicest relationship with her mom; it's so cool. They can talk and everything.

"Anyway, I'd gotten a call from my mom to come home, because it was my older sister's birthday. We were all going out for dinner or something. I went to my sister and I told her that I was pregnant, and you know what she did? She slapped me, real hard in the face! I didn't know it then, but she was pregnant too. She was further along than me, but she didn't show much. I think she slapped me because she was mad—at herself more than at me. Anyhow, she said to me, 'What are you going to do?' And I said I just didn't know."

Safa chose to ignore her boyfriend's faults when she became sexually active with him. Terry had had two other children by two different girls when she met him and "he's had two other kids since my son was born."

"HE CALLED ME A LITTLE TRAMP"

Safa and her older sister endured the birthday celebration, even though they were both sad and preoccupied.

"I went back to Jay's house afterwards to spend the night," Safa says. "And about three in the morning, I couldn't stand it anymore. I called my mom and told her I was pregnant. She didn't really react much then. She just said that I should come home the next day."

If Safa expected support from her parents, she soon found that she would have to look elsewhere.

"My mom wouldn't really even talk about it with me," she says. "I think she'd always expected it of me. She'd always say, 'You're the first of the five that will get yourself pregnant, wait and see.' She was just waiting for it to happen, you know?

"My dad . . . well, his was the reaction I was really dreading. I wasn't so much embarrassed telling him as I was ashamed. I mean, my name means 'purity' and everything. And he was angry, just like I knew he would be. I'd betrayed my name, he said, betrayed him. He called me a little tramp. My sister had also told them about her pregnancy, and he said to my mom, 'What are you running over there, a whorehouse?' That really hurt."

DECISIONS

Safa thought seriously about an abortion but did not go through with it. A large part of that decision, she says, was the money.

"I wanted one," she says. "I didn't have any money, but I asked my mom, and she said she'd talk to my dad. But he was so angry he wouldn't even hear about it, you know? He was like, 'She made her bed, now she'll have to lie in it,' and stuff like that. His idea was that I would have to have the baby and take care of it, and that would be like taking the consequences of my actions. If I didn't want a baby, he said, I should have thought of that before I got myself pregnant."

Safa snorts.

"Get myself pregnant? Right. I sure didn't do that by myself, but you would have thought I did. I told Terry, and he's like, 'Are you sure it's mine?' Really nice, huh? And my parents were the same way. They just said, 'Who cares who the father of the baby is; you probably don't even know yourself!'

"I kept after Terry, and he said he'd get me the money, but he never did. That was all lies, you know. Then after a while, he'd say, 'Did you get that abortion yet?' And I'd say, 'Do I have the money yet?' I told him it was his responsibility, but he didn't care. That's when I really started disliking him—no, hating him."

Safa could not get money from her parents, and Terry was unwilling to help pay for her abortion. She knew she could get the money from Jay's mother, but she was unwilling to do that.

"I knew she'd help me in a minute, she's so nice," Safa says, smiling. "But I couldn't ask her. They didn't have a lot of money either, because Jay's father was on disability, plus they were trying to buy a house. The last thing I wanted to do was to take advantage of them."

So, Safa says, she was resigned to having the baby, although the very idea was frightening to her.

"I didn't have anybody to count on," she says quietly, "and I was having this baby. I couldn't rely on my mom to support us, to

When Mahari was born, Safa had to struggle with the disappointment: "I didn't love him right away. Not at all. I felt kind of guilty, too. I had a feeling something must be wrong for me not to have those feelings."

help me with the baby. She wasn't supporting any of us anymore. I mean, she was so into her crack that she couldn't do anything else.

"I was really depressed, I mean *really* depressed. I knew I couldn't afford this child, and I didn't feel good, either. I thought about adoption, but not for very long. I'd had this one caseworker at Saint Joe's; she'd told me not to put my baby up for adoption. She advised me to keep the baby, and if I needed to, I should put him in a good foster home until I was ready to take care of him. I guess I couldn't just think about giving the baby up. Once abortion wasn't an option anymore, I figured I would keep my baby."

"You Could Just See the Stress in That Baby's Face"

When her son was born, Safa says, she was no more delighted than she had been about the news of her pregnancy.

"I didn't love him right away," she admits. "Not at all. I felt kind of guilty, too. I had a feeling something must be wrong for me not to have those feelings that you'd expect to have when you first see your own child. People told me, though, that he'd grow on me, that it would happen eventually.

"Terry didn't come to the hospital to see me or the baby, and that hurt. I know the baby picked up on all of that hurt, that worry. In every picture you could just see the stress in that baby's face, he was so unhappy. It was like he knew what he was getting into, being born. I was unhappy. It was a miserable time for both of us."

Things got worse when Safa and little Mahari came home from the hospital. The tense relationship between Safa and her mother became even more unbearable.

"Back before Mahari was born, when I was pregnant," says Safa, "my mother's boyfriend, Frank, would hit me, hit my mom. She'd toss him out for a while, and we'd say, 'Mom, don't take him back; he's no good for you,' but she always did.

"Well, it got bad just after I got home from the hospital. My mom had told Frank to get out a little while before. He'd been beating on her again, you know? Well, he's pounding on the door, yelling and cussing, and saying to my mom, 'You're nothing but a crack head; did you tell your kids you're on crack?' And of course, she's denying it, even though I knew it was true.

"Anyway, he ended up coming inside and yelling at my mom. He started punching her, and I just lost it. I mean, I'm in a shirt and robe, just out of the hospital with a brand-new baby, it's January, with lots of snow on the ground. And here is my mother's stupid boyfriend, punching her in the face."

Safa takes a deep breath.

"So I ran and got a knife and went crazy, chasing him with this sharp knife, all the way down this busy street. And I cut him. I didn't really mean to hurt Frank, because I don't agree with hurting people, but I couldn't handle him punching my mom that way, you know. I didn't hurt him bad, not really.

"Anyway, the next day it's more of the same, just like always. Frank is back with my mom; he's telling me he's going to the police to tell them what I've done to him. I mean, this guy never pays rent or anything in my house, but he's basically acting like he runs the place, you know? That's the kind of thing that stressed me out so much when Mahari was first born."

Safa says that financial troubles made her family tensions seem that much more hopeless.

"I couldn't get any welfare, on account of living with my mom. So I lied; I said I was living with somebody else. I look at it like I was doing it to take care of my son, you know? I needed to make sure we had some money. But even that backfired—I'd end up using the welfare money to pay my mom's rent, since she's spending everything she has on drugs for her and her boyfriend. It was a bad, bad time."

"BEING A MOTHER IS SO HARD"

Safa and Mahari moved out of her mother's house more than eighteen months ago. It was a move that Safa knows was necessary but at the same time was frightening.

"It feels strange to be on our own, just the two of us," she admits. "I haven't always been in this apartment—I lived south of here before. Here, it's the 'hood, you know? I mean, it's a great apartment, with great ceilings and plenty of light. But the neighborhood is the worst—prostitutes, people selling drugs right outside."

In addition to worrying about the safety of her neighborhood, Safa has had to come to terms with her own limitations as a mother.

"I have a hard time with love," she says. "I mean, my mother never showed me any. My dad didn't, like I said. Sometimes I think I don't really know how to love Mahari, not really. I mean, I *do* love him, but I'm not always good at showing it.

"I know I'm better than I was. I mean, when he was little, I wasn't really into being a mother at all. It would be like, 'Who wants to watch my son?' I didn't even really care. But I'm more caring now."

But still, Safa says, motherhood is far more difficult than she ever imagined.

"Being a mother is so hard, harder than anybody would think. You have to be so patient; you have to worry all the time about someone being safe, or warm, or fed. And sometimes you just don't have the energy, or the patience.

"I admit sometimes I have had a problem with hitting, getting angry," she says. "I know that. I'm taking parenting classes now for that reason, so I can learn how to be a better mother. I think sometimes that I'm just like my mom—yell, scream, hit. But I don't want to be like that, that's for sure."

I Quit My Job

Until recently Safa was going to school as well as holding down a part-time job in a local discount store. The job gave her the satisfaction of being off welfare and, at the same time, enjoying some extra money for her and Mahari. However, she says, the job caused more problems than it solved.

"I was so tired all the time," she says. "This was the time when I realized I had to get my life under control. I'd go to school, then go to work. I thought I was really accomplishing something, getting off welfare, which I know is a dead end. But after work, when I picked Mahari up from his day care, I was exhausted. The last thing I wanted was to have that child climbing on me, needing me.

"One day I came home from work—I had a headache and I was really tired—I wasn't even thinking. When he came to me, wanting to sit in my lap or wanting me to read to him or something, I just snapped. I said, 'Mahari, leave me the fuck alone!' I mean, I really yelled it."

Safa covers her eyes, remembering.

"I started crying then, because I thought, I'm doing just what my mom used to do to me. And I don't want that; I really don't want to be like that.

"So now I stay home with my son. We have less money, but I'm more awake when I pick him up at 5:30. I'm not always the most relaxed person, but I'm less stressed than I was before, that's for sure."

"You Don't Have a Daddy"

Like most teenage mothers, Safa is raising her son without support—financial or emotional—from the child's father.

"Terry is not a part of my son's life," she says with an edge to her voice. "We see him from time to time, since he's Jay's cousin and hangs around with some of my friends. But he's never done anything to help me or my son.

"Sometimes he likes to take credit for how cute Mahari looks, you know? I mean, his other kids are not as cute as Mahari; in fact, they're kind of ugly. I'm not trying to be mean, you understand, but they just aren't cute.

"So anyway, when I'm out with Mahari, and he's dressed up nice, Terry will show off for his friends. He'll be like, 'Hey, look—my kid's got a new Polo hookup,' or 'Oh, you see my son's new Guess outfit?' Like he had anything to do with how Mahari dresses, you know? He tries to use Mahari like that. Or he'll play this big macho thing and come up to Mahari and say, 'Hey, my man' and that kind of stuff. It just scares Mahari, I think. He doesn't care about Mahari, that's for sure.

"I hear about Terry from Jay's mom. He's in jail right now for murder. I guess the word is that he'll be released soon, since they don't have any evidence. Let him rot, I say."

Safa admits that she has thought about marrying to fill the need for security in her life and a father in Mahari's.

"I sometimes think I should marry a Muslim," she says. "Not for love or anything, just to be married. It would give Mahari some structure, some security that he needs, some guidance and discipline. I mean, I see him with his Power Ranger gun, and he'll point it and say, 'I shoot you in the head!' I hate that, I really do. I don't want him growing up thinking that's the way to be a man.

"I mean, right now it isn't so hard. He'll come up to me sometimes and say, 'Mommy, where's Daddy?' I tell him, 'You don't have a Daddy,' and he'll just say 'Okay.' But I know that he'll get older, and the answers have to be different, you know?"

Speaking Her Mind

Safa says that she has matured in many ways since Mahari's birth, and that maturity makes it more difficult to be silent when her friends are making what she perceives to be mistakes.

Safa receives no support from her baby's father and little from her own family. She worries that Mahari will suffer from the lack of a father and become involved in gang life like his father.

"I speak my mind," she admits. "And that's not always a real popular thing with my friends, I know. I mean, I lose friends over it, if the friends are my same age. I criticize them, and that's maybe a fault. But I do it for the better; I feel like I can see some of the mistakes they're making. They're mistakes I made or I've seen other people make, you know?

"But my friends don't take it like that. We'll be talking on the phone and I'll tell them what they're doing wrong, and they're like, 'Oh, you're being so mean,' and I'm like, 'Oh, whatever, I don't care,' and then I just hang up. I know I've got to learn to be nicer, but it's so hard to watch people doing stuff that they'll regret.

"Jay's a good example. I mean, she's been my friend for a long time. But now she's mad at me, too. I really don't see her much anymore, and I miss her. But she's mad because I disagree with the boyfriend she has. He beats up on her, and I hate that. So I tell her and, well, like I said, I'm not making any friends, you know?"

"I DON'T WANT NO DRUG DEALER"

The maturity Safa has gained has also made her more nervous about the drugs and violence that permeate her neighborhood and the school she attends.

"I've never been interested in drugs," she says firmly. "Never. They scare me—not only what they can do to your body, but the kind of things that happen to you when you get involved with drug dealers. My cousin is into crack so bad. He and his wife are always strung out. Last week some dealers beat him up. I guess he owed them money or something. But he's having brain surgery because of the beating he took.

"So many of the people at school, kids I used to hang out with, are so into drugs, especially weed. You know, marijuana. Everything's weed, weed, weed. Unless you're doing weed, you're not cool. And blunts . . . everybody talks about blunts. They're cigars with the insides taken out and filled with marijuana, like a giant joint. Kids are like, 'Can I get a blunt for this?' or 'Will you trade me a blunt for that?' It's so stupid."

Especially frightening to Safa is the apparent ease with which so many people her age are willing to sell drugs instead of getting real jobs. Boys who she knows are dealing drugs have asked her out, but Safa will have none of that.

"I don't want drugs, any of that, in my son's life. At all. I don't want no drug dealer. So they have lots of money, their girlfriends don't have to work. So what, I say. I'd rather work. I've told these boys, 'You don't appreciate what you have, because it comes so quick.' There's no value to anything. I mean, I appreciate my money, and I wouldn't spend a dime on their stupid weed or whatever. I'd rather buy something for my son or get something we both can enjoy."

"All They Want to Do Is Fight and Kill"

Racial hostility is another thing that infuriates Safa. Racism is a fact of life, she says, but there is a dangerous mood among the people she knows that scares her.

"I'm half black," she says, "and I love being around black people. But the kids at the school I went to last year are so ignorant, so ghetto. All they want to do is fight and kill and talk about who they're going to go after—stuff like that.

"And they're into so much excusing, putting the blame on other people for their own failure. I mean, you hear so many of those kids saying, 'I can't do this or that because of the white people.' Hey, they have to get over that, you know? I mean, you want to amount to anything, you have to get over that, do what's best for you.

"But there are so many kids at my school who are so worried about what the white man isn't letting them do or what the white man did to black people hundreds of years ago, it's so stupid to keep it up. They're lying anyway; I tell them that. I say, 'No, the reason you don't have nothing is because you're not trying.'"

Safa recently broke up with a boy she'd been seeing because of his racial attitudes. Their trouble, she says, started over an incident that happened at a nearby high school in which a white boy was killed over some fancy tire rims on his car.

"The police figure those rims were worth five or six hundred dollars apiece," she explains, "and somebody wanted them. My boyfriend acted like he maybe knew who killed the boy. I asked him why he didn't say anything to the police. He's like, 'It's none of our business; and the boy was white anyway.'

"I said, 'That's so ignorant. Why should that boy have to give up his stuff to other kids, when it's his and he paid for it?'"

Safa shakes her head in disgust.

"You see what I mean? He's ignorant; he's stupid. I mean, when you think about it, it isn't really about race anyway, it's just about common sense. I told my boyfriend, 'You're not my boyfriend, you're stupid. I'm getting my number changed.' Like that. I just can't believe how people think."

I'VE GOT SOME IDEAS

Safa says that she plans on returning in the fall to the school at which she started her high school career. Although it has problems, too, she feels that the school is better for her.

"I think the kids are more together there," she says. "Everybody pushes each other to graduate or reminds each other to sign up for this scholarship or that placement test, or whatever. I like that. The kids really try to work together. At my other school it was just fights—three or four big fights every day.

"I've got to look ahead. I am going to graduate this year, that's for sure. I've had problems in the past, not with learning, but just getting to class. Once I'm there, I'm okay. But sometimes Mahari is sick. Or maybe I'm so depressed about things that I don't want to see nobody. And that gets so hard, you know, doing it all yourself. That's where it would help to have a second parent there, helping. Girls who get pregnant and have the baby's father around . . . that would really be a help."

Safa says that after graduation she plans on going to college. She has already filled out an application for a scholarship to a local college that has a good education department.

"I'd like to be an eleventh-grade history teacher," she says with a smile. "I had such a good one last year—the only good thing about school last year, as a matter of fact. That teacher was so good, especially when it came to teaching about the civil rights movement in this country. He changed my life, really opened up my mind.

"I did really good work for him, too," she says proudly. "In fact, he told me I really should be going to college. It was such a change, having somebody believe in me that way. It would be nice to be a teacher that could do things like that for kids."

THE HERE AND NOW

Talking about the future puts a light in Safa's eyes. For a few minutes she talks with enthusiasm of the courses she would like to take, the kind of colleges she is interested in. But the real world for her is today, and it seems to her neither glamorous nor exciting.

"My life is pretty dull," says Safa. "I mean, there is such a routine to the first part of the day. We get up early, and as soon as he's up we are arguing because he wants a cookie. I mean, every day, it's the same argument. He eats his cereal, watches a little Lamb Chop on TV, then we're off. School, day care—that's the routine.

Safa is struggling to get her degree, and the support of her history teacher makes her think that she could go further: "It was such a change, having somebody believe in me that way."

"When we come home, we go to the park, and he swings or plays there."

Safa rolls her eyes, interrupting herself.

"God, I'm so tired of going to the park. I know Mahari likes it, especially when he knows I'm watching him do something. But I'm bored with it; I don't like it anymore.

"Anyway, he comes home, watches TV or a tape. He likes his VCR—or at least he did before he stuck the cheese in it. We eat dinner then it's time to clean up some mess that he's made. He goes to bed; but doesn't like it unless I come in and lie down with him for a while. He falls asleep, then in the night comes into my room and gets in bed with me. That's a typical day, really. Same thing, day after day."

Safa closes her eyes a moment. When she opens them again, she looks extraordinarily weary.

"It is just . . . so hard," she says, shaking her head at her inability to find the right words. "I just get so afraid that he's going to end up bad, that I won't be strong enough for him. I think, am I raising him to be a good boy? I see him with those Power Ranger things, those guns or whatever. I mean, he thinks he's Mr. Man, and I don't want him to be like that. I like him better when he's sweet and nice. He can be that way, too."

"I'd Undo Mahari"

When asked if there were anything in her life that she would undo or change if she could, Safa does not hesitate.

"I'd undo Mahari. I really would, in a minute. I love him, but I still don't really feel that I can ever really give him a good life. Seriously, I like to think that I could go to college and be this great teacher, and get a nice house, and we'd have a life.

"But do I really think I'm strong enough to do that? I mean, I'm still getting help myself. I know from the parenting classes I take that these young years in Mahari's life are so important. I can't wait until he's twelve or thirteen and start doing right by him. That's too late. I feel like I didn't do things right when he was first born, I was so confused. And now things are just hard.

"I love him, though. He's my strength. He's the reason I'm frustrated, but he's the reason I am working so hard at my life right now. He's the only thing that keeps me on this earth. I sure can't say that about anybody else. I'd do anything to protect him, to keep him from harm."

Safa smiles weakly.

"But still, I am not happy, not at all. My life is not how I wanted it to be. Maybe it will get better; I'm not giving up or anything. I mean, my dad has changed from the way he was when I was little. He's realizing he was too cold, too strict. That's a start. I'm looking forward to Mahari getting to know him.

"And my mom . . . well, she still has lots of problems. She's been through treatment, and she's not using drugs, but she still has Frank. He's messed up our family so much, I wish she'd lose him. They even told her at treatment that it would be harder for her to have him around. He's no good influence on her, that's for sure. But Mahari likes his grandma, and I guess that's another start.

"But anybody who thinks having a baby when they're still in high school will be fun is crazy. It's the hardest thing in the world, in the whole world."

Lisa

"WHEN I GOT THE RESULTS, AND THEY TOLD ME I WAS PREGNANT, I JUST GOT NUMB. . . . I PRETTY MUCH EXPECTED IT. BUT TO HEAR THE WORDS MADE IT KIND OF OFFICIAL."

There are thirty-eight steep steps going up to the apartment. It's on the third floor, above the Oriental Grocery. The neighborhood is obviously deteriorating; many storefronts that once housed bookstores and gift shops catering to a university crowd are now deserted. A low-income high-rise is across the street from the grocery, and gang graffiti is splashed on every surface—buildings, mailboxes, bus shelters. It is 11:30 in the morning, and early-bird crack dealers stare sullenly at passersby.

There are no buzzers or phones for visitors to call from downstairs to the apartments above the grocery. It's especially difficult to reach sixteen-year-old Lisa, because her phone has recently been disconnected.

"I'm sorry about that," says Lisa, holding a dark-eyed baby as she braces the heavy door open. "They just shut off the phone yesterday. I'd run up a big phone bill—about two hundred dollars—and I've been trying to pay it off a little at a time, but I couldn't keep up with the payments.

"Next time, if you need to get in touch with me," she suggests, "you can stand under my window and yell. My window is right under that light pole, the window with the fan. Just yell, and I'll usually hear you."

Lisa is quiet, but it is a quiet that comes less from shyness than wariness. She lives with her nearly two-year-old son, Domanick, in this third-floor walkup. Dan, Domanick's father, lies on the sofa in the stuffy apartment, trying to cool off in front of the fan.

"I Feel Like a Native"

Lisa is used to the area; she says that with the exception of her first few years, her family has always lived in Minneapolis.

"I've lived in this neighborhood almost all my life," she says. "I was born up north, in Bemidji [Minnesota]. I lived there until I was five, but then we came down here. My mother was young when she had me—seventeen, I think. She and my father had met when he was a student in a college up there; she was in high school."

Lisa has a darker complexion than most other Native Americans, she says, because her father was a mixture of black and Korean. But since she was raised by her mother, she has always considered herself a Native American first, an Ojibwa, like her mother.

"Once or twice my heritage has started some problems," she says. "In junior high there was this one black girl who got on me because I was hanging around with all Native friends. She said to me, 'How come you're hanging with Indians when you're black?' She was upset, like she wanted to teach me a lesson or something.

"But I feel like a Native; I go to an Indian school, all my friends are Natives. In fact, I didn't even know I was part black until I was nine. I have two younger brothers and a younger sister, and I'd always called their father Dad. Maybe I knew it down inside; I don't really remember."

"We Got to Go Take Some Blood Tests"

"Anyway, when I was nine, my mom comes in and says to me, 'We got to go take some blood tests.' I asked her what for. She told me that my real dad wants to know if I'm really his, and she showed me a picture of him.

"I don't really remember what I thought about the whole thing," she admits. "I think it was kind of weird, finding out like that, that I was his and he was mine. I do remember that right after that, we started visiting each other. I went down to Oceanside, California, where he lived during the summer, and he'd come up here, too.

"It was strange going out there, flying on an airplane and everything. He had a family; it was weird to find out I had a sister who's six and an eleven-month-old brother."

Lisa stops talking abruptly, takes a deep breath.

"My dad died just a couple of months ago, in June," she says quietly. "He had leukemia. He wasn't quite forty. I wish he'd been able to know Domanick; I had plans to bring him to California to meet his grandpa. My dad would have liked him.

"I called him from the hospital, told him about Domanick being born. But we never made it to California. I went myself for the fu-

Lisa had Domanick at age fourteen. At sixteen, she has taken on the adult responsibilities of motherhood and taking care of her own apartment.

neral, but I couldn't see bringing a little kid, chasing him around at something like that, you know?"

"She Just Couldn't Handle Me"

Although she says that her early childhood was mostly happy, Lisa admits that she got "kind of wild" after grade school.

"I started messing up when I got into middle school," she says. "I was wild, skipping school, getting into all kinds of trouble. When I was twelve or so, that's when it started.

"I'd take the bus to school—I'd start the day off like I was going to be good—then I'd go to first-hour class and meet my friends. We'd take off then, maybe go downtown, hang out at the IDS skyscraper, go to the fiftieth floor and look out the windows. We got chased sometimes, but usually no big problem."

Looking back, Lisa says, her mom could have prevented a lot of the trouble by being more firm, more consistent in her discipline.

"I mean, she was home all the time," says Lisa. "It wasn't like she didn't know what was going on because she was at work or something. She just couldn't handle me; she would just send me away. I'd go to my aunt's or uncle's to live when she couldn't manage me. I ran wild, I admit it.

"My mom wouldn't be scared of me, just mad. But she didn't know how to discipline me. She'd ground me sometimes, but then I'd leave, and she wouldn't do nothing about it. She wasn't strict enough, didn't make sure the punishment stuck.

"I wouldn't listen; I'd stay gone weeks at a time. Then I'd come home for a little while, just long enough to eat, sleep, change my clothes, maybe do a little housework for my mom. Then I'd be gone again for a couple more days.

"Sometimes," she says, "I'd stay at friends' houses. Their parents knew I was there, and I wasn't snotty or nothing, so they let me stay. I'd help out there, too. I just wasn't happy at my house. I didn't like it at home, not at all."

Safe at Home

Lisa maintains that she grew up earlier than many of her peers, mainly because of the fast lifestyle she adopted when she was young.

"When I was real little, up north, I didn't have a care in the world," she says. "And even when I was between eight and ten, things were okay. I mean, that was when I started drinking and smoking and stuff, but I wasn't really running wild, not like later on."

Lisa says that while she considers herself a moderate drinker now, she has cut down a lot from when she was younger. In fact, she says, smiling, it was her mother that got her started.

"I was nine, I think," she says, squinting to remember. "Back then I was a real tomboy, hanging around with a crowd of boys, having fun. I was fooling around, and asked my mom if me and my friends could have a party, have some beer. I was just messing around; I never thought she'd say okay.

"But she was willing! She said, 'Give me the money then.' I said, 'For real?' I couldn't believe it, man. So, eight of us kids chipped in for a case of Old Milwaukee, and my mom went up to the store to get it for us. She just said that she didn't want us to get too drunk. We did, though."

Lisa says that her mother was adamant that if her daughter was going to drink, she'd rather have her drinking at home than in a bar or in a park somewhere.

"It was the same on my eleventh birthday," she says. "My mom got me a case of beer and a gallon of Windsor whiskey. I got drunk, but she didn't mind. At least, she said, I'd be safe there at home."

"Our Family's Been Through Some Hell Because of Him"

Lisa says that her family was getting along for the most part until her mother split up with her younger siblings' father.

"I feel bad that they didn't stay together," she says. "Like I said, when I was younger, he was like a father to me, too. But he was an epileptic and had seizures all the time. My mom couldn't handle the seizures, taking him to the hospital, back and forth.

"So she said, we got to break up. That's what she told him. And that's where Jaime came in; he's her boyfriend now. Our family's been through some hell because of him, that's for sure. I hate him, and he knows it."

Lisa says that her mother never drank heavily until she met Jaime, but now her mother drinks more than he does.

"I was eleven when they started living together," she says. "At first he wasn't so bad. I mean, they'd start drinking, and I'd leave.

That was one of the reasons I was gone so much from my house. But even though they'd be drinking, Jaime wouldn't be so bad. He was pretty nice to start out with, but as I got older...."

Lisa shakes her head in disgust.

"I just despise him. He's kind of a rough guy. He's big, and he thinks he's really something because of that. We've gotten into some physical fights, me and him.

"One time I'd been at my friend's house. I came home to get some clothes or something, and my mom wasn't home. Jaime was there, though. I went up to my room to grab a sweatshirt or something, and he wouldn't let me leave. He was really drunk then.

"He said, 'Your mom isn't here, and I'm not going to let you go anywhere.' I told him I wasn't staying there with him, that my friends were outside waiting for me. I was really mad—I was kicking him and stuff, trying to get by him, but he wouldn't move. I went to the window and yelled for my friends to come up and help me because Jaime wouldn't let me out. He tried to shut the window on my neck, but I ran out the door."

Lisa says that he pushed her into a downstairs bathroom. If it hadn't been for her friends, she says, he would certainly have hurt her.

"My friends grabbed his leg, and they pulled him," she says. "He fell down the stairs. I started punching him and kicking him. Like I said, he wasn't real steady on his feet because he'd been drinking. Anyway, I ran out, and I got free."

It was not the only time he'd threatened her, she says.

"Another time I got beat up at a party my mom was having," says Lisa. "One of my mom's friends asked me for a cigarette. I didn't have one, and she got mad. She pushed me, and I pushed her back. Well, Jaime was standing nearby, and thought I'd pushed my mother. So he's like, 'Don't you ever do that,' and he jumped on me and started banging my head against the floor. Someone pushed him off me, or I would have been hurt worse than I was. I hate him, like I said."

GETTING PREGNANT

It was in her freshman year of high school that Lisa became pregnant, although, she says, Dan was not the first boy she had had sex with. He was three years older than she, and they had met through friends.

"I had been with a couple of other boys," she says, trying not to smile as she glanced sideways at Dan. "My mom didn't even know I was going out with Dan; she wouldn't have cared anyway. It was funny, because she was always worried about me being a tomboy, like I wasn't going to be interested in boys. I think when she found out about my first boyfriend, she was relieved."

Lisa says that although she had been sexually active, she had never seriously thought about birth control.

"I'm on it now," she says with a laugh. "I guess that's backwards, right? But I never really thought about it. I don't know

Lisa's mother did not take her caretaking responsibilities seriously. Lisa admits that her mother was an inconsistent, if incompetent, disciplinarian and allowed her young daughter to drink beer at her ninth birthday party.

what I was thinking, I really don't. But anyway, I got pregnant in December, or early January.

"I knew I was pregnant," she says. "I just went to get the test to make sure. I was really tired all the time. I'd get up in the morning, get dressed, and go right back to sleep. I felt kind of sick. But I didn't tell anybody right away; I don't think I was ready to do that. Besides, you can't trust many people with secrets like that."

Going to the Clinic

Lisa recalls being quite unafraid when she went to the clinic for her pregnancy test. She was, however, a little worried because she was a minor and didn't have a parent with her.

"They weren't going to take me at the Indian Health Board, since my mom wasn't there," she remembers. "I didn't have a slip or anything that was signed by a parent. So I had to tell them a big old lie.

"When they told me I had to go home to have a permission slip signed, I told them that my mother was working and I couldn't reach her," smiles Lisa. "I told them she was cleaning a house, and I had no idea what the phone number was. Really, I just didn't want to have her come with me. I don't know why.

"The clinic people asked if I couldn't come back tomorrow, but I told them no, that this was the only time I could come in. So they gave in. I sat there for ten minutes while I waited for the results. While I was waiting, this nurse talked to me about the possibilities—what I'd do if it were positive, stuff like that.

"But then, when I got the results, and they told me I was pregnant, I just got numb. I felt numb, my whole body," she says. "It's funny, since I pretty much expected it. But to hear the words made it kind of official, and I don't think I was prepared."

A Traumatic Time

Lisa says that she told her mother right away, and her mother was angry.

"She was mad, yes," Lisa says. "I walked up to the house when she and Jaime were sitting outside. She asked me what I was doing home from school so early, and I told her that I had good and bad news. But before I could say anything, Jaime says, 'You're pregnant, huh?' Just like that. I said 'Yep.' And mom, she didn't talk to me for about two weeks."

It was during her pregnancy that the problems between Jaime and Lisa's brothers and sister escalated—a situation that put a lot of stress on Lisa.

"The younger kids told the authorities that Jaime had molested them," she says. "They hated him so much, for beating on my mom and for being mean to them—all the drinking and everything. I guess they thought that if they told that, they could get him kicked out. Maybe they thought things would be better.

"I don't think Jaime did anything sexual, but he sure was mean. Anyway, when I was about seven months along, the police came to the house. It was early, like six in the morning. We were all sleeping, and the officers woke us up, told us we had to leave.

"Jaime had taken off; he knew there was going to be trouble, I think. But my mom had been drinking the night before, and one of the officers thought her breath smelled like she was drunk that morning. It was just morning breath, though. But he said it was 'the stench of beer,' like she'd been drinking all night."

THE FIGHT

"And then another thing happened," says Lisa tentatively. "In the process of doing all of this, the police found that there was a warrant out for my arrest."

A warrant?

Lisa rolls her eyes.

"I had punched this one girl at the school where I used to go," she says. "She pressed charges. I never got no court papers or nothing; I never heard anything about it until that morning.

"It was a stupid fight. We had been out waiting for our bus after school. She was talking shit, you know, saying I wasn't nothing, that I couldn't do nothing to her. She wasn't too big—same size as me. Anyway, I went right up to her and told her she was talking shit, which she was.

"She said, 'I ain't talking shit.' And so I slapped her once, and she didn't do anything, so I uppercut her. She went running into the school, and next thing you know, the principal comes running out and grabs me. The girl's cheek was all red, you know, and bruised—really swelling up.

"The principal said, 'Oh, look what you did; now we'll have to take her to the hospital.' I didn't really care. I lost my temper a lot back then. So that was the whole fight, and the end of it, I thought."

Foster Homes and the Juvenile Center

Lisa realized how wrong she was when the officers took her to JC, the juvenile center. Her brothers and sister were taken to emergency foster care.

"JC is like a jail," she explains. "I was so surprised. It had been seven or eight months since I punched her. But there I was, going off to the jail. Little cells where they lock you up.

"I stayed there for two days, and then they told me they were planning to put me in foster homes, just like they put my brothers and sister. But man, I didn't want to be in no foster home—I was pregnant! But they took me to an emergency foster home, and I got busy scheming on a way to get out of there."

Her opportunity came within a few days. She informed the people at the foster home that she had a prenatal appointment, an appointment that she could not miss.

"They tried to talk me out of it," says Lisa. "They said they had a nurse there at the emergency foster home, that she could help me. But I made up a story about how I had to see my own doctor, since I was due in just eight weeks or so.

"They drove me to the Indian Health Board, where I told them my appointment was. They said to call when I was done and they'd pick me up. As soon as they left, I was gone. I have friends all over in the neighborhood; there's lots of Natives around there.

"I ended up being rescued by my friend Julie's mother. Her name is Laurie, and she's really great. She told me I shouldn't be on the run, that it wasn't good for me or the baby. And I told her I didn't want to be in no foster home, not being pregnant.

"She ended up becoming my foster mother. She went through all the paperwork and everything. She did a lot, and she has six kids of her own! I stayed there while I was pregnant and even after Domanick was born."

"I Loved Him Right Away"

Her foster home was just three or four blocks from her mother's house, however, and Lisa found herself going back for visits, especially as her due date approached.

"I don't know how I felt about her," admits Lisa. "I mean, I was sort of mad at her for being with Jaime and because she was so loyal to him. But, also, I was pregnant, and I wanted my mom around, you know?

"In fact, the night before I went into the hospital, I had been over at my mom's for dinner. The next morning—real early, like two o'clock—I started having contractions. I sat up all night, timing how far apart they were. When they were close enough to go to the hospital, Laurie didn't have a car, so she called a friend who did. She and her niece went, plus Laurie—a whole bunch of us."

Domanick was born at 1:30 that afternoon, and Lisa says she was very, very happy.

"Yeah, of course I was happy," she smiles. "I didn't care if it was a girl or boy, just so it came out of me, man. He was really cute, and I loved him right away. My mom gave him his name, Domanick. He's named after one of my uncles who died in a house fire up north, when he was just eighteen months old. His middle name is Cody—I named him that, because I liked the sound of it. He stayed right in my room while I was in the hospital, right by me. I'll always remember him snoring, when he was only a couple of hours old."

Lisa rolls her eyes as she remembers the nurses in the hospital asking if she'd like to take parenting classes.

"It wasn't like they just asked," she snorts. "They kept asking me like every hour. Do you want to take parenting classes? Would you like to attend? I think it was because I was a Native, or because I was a teenager, I'm not sure. But no, I didn't want to.

"Hey, I've been baby-sitting since I was six—my little brother when my mom went to town, or my little cousin when my aunt went to bingo, or whatever. Those parenting classes, they're for . . . well, you know, mostly it's white people.

"No offense," she says, grinning.

"I Hope Domanick Doesn't Get into the Stuff I Was In"

Dan has roused himself from the sofa and sits up sleepily. He is a husky nineteen-year-old, with a quick smile and a drawl that sounds almost southern.

"I've been told I sound like I'm from New Orleans or something," he says. "But I'm not; I've lived here all my life. I'm a mix—Native and Irish. I think I picked up that southern way of talking out on the streets, you know. I've been hanging on the streets with my friends a long time."

Dan was raised on the north side of the city, but because of some trouble in his high school there, he has been going to school up north.

"I was with a gang," he says, "the Gangster Disciples. I got into it big, got a gang tattoo and everything. But when I went into the system, you know, the juvenile center and stuff like that, I was warned that it wasn't no good to have a gang sign like that. See this big scar? That's where I had it taken off."

In spite of her mother's poor skills, Lisa felt competent to take on the responsibility of motherhood right away: "Hey, I've been baby-sitting since I was six—my little brother when my mom went to town, or my little cousin when my aunt went to bingo."

"I hope Domanick doesn't get into the stuff I was in—lockup facilities, treatment, stuff like that. I made mistakes, getting into all that gang stuff. At first, when I got locked up, got into the system, I thought the counselors and everyone were really unfair. I thought they weren't respecting me because of all the punishments and stuff. But now, I look back and I think they were making sense. Maybe it's that I got a son now, and I see it different.

"I was a thug, got locked up a lot. Hell, I was locked up when I found out Domanick was born. Either in the lockup, or in treatment."

He looks at Lisa.

"Do you remember where you found me back then?"

Lisa says, "Wasn't it when you were stealing that car, remember, riding around out in Granite Falls?"

Dan nods.

"Yeah, that's right, the 1992 Taurus. Me and my friend took it; we got drunk and I showed him how to steal a car real easy. Anyway, we were driving around, joyriding, and the state troopers picked us up."

Did he sell the cars he stole?

"No, never did," Dan says, shaking his head. "I had my mom to give me money, I was just stealing the cars, just riding in them. My mom gave me sixty or seventy dollars when she had it, so I didn't need to sell no cars."

"I'M AT AN AGE NOW WHERE I CAN LOOK BACK"

"I'm at an age now where I can look back," says Dan, "and I can see that if I'd stayed on the road I was on, I would have been dead or in prison. Lots of banging around, you know. I carried a pistol—more for frontin' [showing other people that he couldn't be taken advantage of] because of the other people I was around. I don't think of myself as a violent person, but back then, if I was in a crowd of five or six of my friends and they said 'Shoot,' I probably would have. That would have been my state of mind, you know what I'm talking about?"

Dan says his mother had been worried about his involvement with gangs, too, not only for his safety, but for the example Dan set for his two younger sisters.

"My sisters are little—four and nine," he says. "And that was a sore point between my mom and me. My sisters were into imitat-

Domanick's father, Dan, was heavily involved in gangs. "I don't think of myself as a violent person, but back then, if I was in a crowd of five or six of my friends and they said 'Shoot,' I probably would have."

ing me, learning all that gang stuff, dressing like gangsters, throwing those gang signs, stuff like that.

"My mom came to me and said, 'You're not setting no good example. My little girls are going to get their asses kicked, acting like you.' And she was right, you know. I know that now, but it took me a long time to see that. That's what I worry about, Domanick growing up and trying to act tough like that; it's no good.

"I got another kid, you know—a daughter. It feels strange, having two kids. I mean, I wasn't mad or nothing when Lisa told me she was pregnant. Hey, I know it takes two to tango, you know?

"The other woman isn't living a good life. She's got problems, using inhalants, stuff like that. She's from up north. I saw her like three weeks ago, and asked her where she's living. She said, 'Everywhere.' She's like living on the streets, not doing so good. And the little girl, she's three, just turned three last month. Man, that makes me feel weird."

"You Don't Have No Friends"

Dan says that it was a talk that his mother had with him that got him to start changing his life.

"I was locked up this last time," he says, "and my mom was visiting me. She says, 'You know, they say that when you're down and out, your best friends are the ones that stick by you.' And she says, 'So, Dan, where are your friends?'

"I told her they're all on the outside, not in the lockup. She asked me, 'Do any of them call you?' I said 'No.' She said, 'Do any of them write you?' I said 'No.' She said, 'Then you don't have no friends, simple as that.'

I said, 'Shoot.' And you know, I really thought about what she said. I thought about it a lot."

So Dan is finishing high school up north, he says, away from the pressures of the city streets.

"I got lots of aunts and uncles up there, they keep me. I get along good with them, have friends up there. I play football for my high school football team, too—the Silver Eagles. Our colors are silver and blue. The guys on the team call me Cop Runner because I'm from the city and because they think I'm tough, I guess.

"But I think I'll do better up there. They got classes up there for people with learning disabilities. That's what I got. I want to get some kind of smarts, but I need special help. I'd like to enlist in the marines after high school, you know? Maybe get a job with the Department of Natural Resources after that, working outside, doing forestry work. I'm good at that, good at working with animals.

"Yeah, I'm sure I'll be doing better up north, won't get into no trouble like here. There are gangs, yeah, but they're more like wanna-bes, you know? Nothing like here in the city.

"Plus, my uncle's a truancy officer," he laughs, "so I got to be good."

Is marriage to Lisa in his future? He looks sideways at Lisa, who smiles.

"I want to, I really do," he says. "We're spending more time together than ever, you know. I'm here for the summer; I'm not in no lockup. It's really different, you know, getting used to being together so often. But I like it. It's my first time living with somebody. I got a son, I got a woman, I got a place to live."

He shrugs, a little self-consciously.

"I like it, I do. From what I understand, she likes it, too. But she's at a young age, she don't want to get married yet. She's got school and everything, but when she finishes up, maybe we will."

"Things Are Still Hard with My Mom"

Since Dan will be leaving in a few days for school, Lisa says she is quite ready to be the full-time parent for their son.

"I know I'll be raising Domanick; I know I can do that," she says. "Things are more complicated where I'm going to be than where Dan will be."

She fishes a cigarette out of a rumpled pack and lights it.

"Things are still hard with my mom. She has the younger kids back—she had to go to treatment and stuff before she could have them. And like I said before, Jaime made himself scarce, so he never got caught.

"She had to tell the courts all kinds of good things about Jaime before the kids could come back. She told them that he hadn't really molested them. But man, we hate him—all of us kids. He beats on my mom, acts real big all the time.

Lisa enjoys parenthood: "Yeah, I do like it. Even though it gets frustrating a lot, especially when I was younger . . . . It's hard to keep your temper down."

"Just recently he's been hiding out. My mom put him in jail one night because he was beating on my little brother, Eddie. I guess he was choking Eddie and punching him. They went to court, and Jaime was supposed to be taking these frustration classes, you know, to control your anger? But he wasn't showing up. And he violated his probation, since he didn't call in or nothing. Now the detectives are looking for him."

She takes a deep drag of her cigarette.

"I hope they find him, I really do. I feel bad that I'm here, living away from home, and the little kids are still there. Jaime is such an asshole, he makes life miserable for them all. The sad thing for my mom is that it puts her in a weird place. She loves him, I guess. But if she had to choose, I think she'd choose him over those kids. I mean, she kind of had to call the cops on Jaime that one time; otherwise, who knows, he might have killed Eddie. But if she had a choice someday, she'd choose Jaime, I'm pretty sure.

"Eddie has turned into a hermit and stays in his room all the time when Jaime is around. Whenever he comes out, he gets bitched at. And my little sister, Rachel, is afraid of him, too. In fact, whenever there is a knock at their door, she's always saying, 'I bet it's Child Protection!' What a way to grow up, huh?"

BEING A PARENT

Lisa had moved back in with her mother when Domanick was just a few months old. However, she realized that the arrangement was not for the best.

"I talked my mom into letting me get my own grant," says Lisa. "I didn't want to be covered under her social security or welfare, or whatever. I wanted to get a check myself—for me and the baby—so we moved out. See, it was hard, with me being only sixteen, because I was a minor, and she would get the money. Lots of times I didn't get much for me and Domanick.

"I moved into the basement of a friend of mine. Me and Domanick stayed there for about a year, then moved into this place. It's not the greatest, but it's okay for now. At least I'm on my own, and I like that."

Although she admits parenting is hard work, Lisa says that most of the time she likes it.

"Yeah, I do like it," she says with a smile. "Even though it gets frustrating a lot, especially when I was younger. Even now, man, my temper's really short. It's hard to keep your temper down, you know? I hit him sometimes, and sometimes I really do spank him pretty hard."

Dan rumples his son's hair.

"But it don't faze him, though," he says proudly.

"I get really frustrated with him when he comes back from visiting at my mom's," Lisa says. "That's when I really get the maddest, I think. She spoils him big-time, and when he comes home to me, I pay for it. He whines—not cries, but makes that awful whining sound—every time he wants something.

"Hey," Lisa explains, "Domanick is capable of talking, of telling what he wants. He knows how to say please, or ask nicely. But not that other stuff, that whining. That's what he does at my mom's, I think."

Lisa and her mother have a difficult and sometimes competitive relationship: "When he comes back from there, he calls me Lisa, not Mommy. I hate that. And I know my mom is teaching him that: she gets him to call her Mom and me Lisa."

She lights another cigarette and moves the ashtray out of reach of Domanick.

"And plus, when he comes back from there, he calls me Lisa, not Mommy. I hate that. And I know my mom is teaching him that: she gets him to call her Mom and me Lisa. She even gets Domanick to call Jaime Dad! That really makes me mad; makes Dan mad, too. Even when I'm over there, she'll pull that shit—do it right in front of me. She'll say to him, 'Say Lisa' and she'll point to me. I don't know why she does that."

Dan looks angry.

"I told her once," he says, 'hey, you had a chance to raise your kids, and your chance is over. It's time now to let us have our chance, you know?'"

"He Just Looked Lifeless"

There are fun parts about raising Domanick, too, Lisa says.

"I love to watch him grow, watch him learn things," she says smiling. "I like making him happy. He's a good kid. He likes to be active, likes to run. I wish we had kids in the building that he could play with, but there's no backyard or anything. We just take him with us most of the time, wherever we're going."

Dan chuckles. "Sometimes it's not too convenient, you know? Like the other day, we took him to a movie. It was pretty dark, and we thought he was sitting between us, you know, in the seat. Well, he wasn't there; he had disappeared. He was sitting in the aisle, just sitting there all by himself. He wasn't scared or nothing, but I was, for a minute."

Lisa says that the most difficult time so far has been when Domanick was sick with pneumonia the winter before.

"It was around January, February—the time when kids get colds and fevers," she explains. "I thought he had a regular old fever; I was giving him Tylenol and stuff. Anyway, the next morning, he didn't get up.

"Now, Domanick's real active," she says. "He usually gets right up in the morning and wakes me up for breakfast. But he didn't do that. He just lay there. He had the same bottle I put in bed with him the night before; he hadn't touched it. I said, man, what's going on?

"I took him to the hospital to be seen, and he ended up being there a week. They had a hard time getting an IV in him, he was so dehydrated. He didn't want to drink a bottle or anything, he just lay there. He just looked lifeless, you know?"

"She Tries to Be Both of Our Ma's"

Lisa says that although she had tried to do everything right for Domanick when he was ill, her mother acted as though Lisa was irresponsible in the care of her son.

"She just got on me, like it was my fault," says Lisa bitterly. "I had been at the hospital for three days straight. Didn't really eat anything except a bag of chips once in a while, you know? I didn't sleep except in a chair by Domanick's bed.

"Anyway, I went home to change. I had to do that. In fact, the doctor told me I could go for longer if I wanted, since Domanick was sleeping so much. But I didn't want to be gone too long—just long enough to grab something to eat, change clothes, get something to do while I was at the hospital. I left that night, while he was sleeping.

"But my mom yelled at me when she found out. She said that I had no right to leave his side."

Lisa says with emotion, "She tries to be both our ma's. She calls all the time, checking to make sure I'm doing everything right. Like last week, Domanick had a runny nose. She's calling, saying, 'You take him in to the doctor's yet?' Like I'm too stupid to take him in when he's sick. I wish she'd just act like she trusted me. I'm doing fine."

"It's Hard to Look Too Far Ahead"

Neither Lisa nor Dan enjoy thinking too much about Domanick's future. They know that some parents like to daydream about the paths their children will someday take, but they do not.

"It's hard to look too far ahead for me, let alone Domanick," protests Lisa. "I don't think about him as a grown-up man, or even as a teenager. I can't predict what he'll do or what kinds of things he'll be interested in, so why try?"

Dan disagrees somewhat; he thinks that there are important lessons for his son to learn so that his growing up is not as painful as his own has been.

"I want him to know that reality is tough," he says. "Enjoy his childhood for a little while, but after that, things get mean. Like me, for instance. We were always poor. Food-shelf food, free school lunches. That's the way it was. Just because I wanted not to be poor didn't mean anything. You can't change reality. That's what Domanick is going to find out when he's older."

Lisa nods, agreeing.

"I don't want Domanick to think he has to have expensive things to be happy. I hope he doesn't get into the same kind of trouble I got into or Dan did. That isn't good, you know? I worry a little, though, because there is so much of that trouble out there, waiting to happen."

LISA'S FUTURE

Her own future is uncertain, says Lisa, but she feels more in control of it than of Domanick's. School is a priority right now, and she is proud that she has become active in her high school.

Lisa met her own father for the first time as an older child. It was the first time she was treated as a dependent child: "It was so weird. . . . He wouldn't let me smoke or drink. He acted like I was a little girl—called me 'baby.'"

"I'm like on the board of directors. We make lots of decisions that the faculty considers," she says. "The school is for Native kids, and so everybody has real similar backgrounds. Except...."

She giggles.

"One time, at school, they had this video called The *Miracle of Birth*. It had the egg and the little sperms, you know? And the boys in the class are like, what is that stuff? These were high school boys, man, and they didn't even know what that stuff was about! Big street kids, they were. It was sort of funny. I said, 'Man, you guys don't know nothing; you need some sex ed.' So anyway, I brought that up at the board meeting, told the people we needed some class so kids would know this stuff."

Lisa thinks that she would like to pursue a career after high school—a dream that she says surprises many of her friends with small children.

"I don't get why everybody thinks my son stops me from going to school, from having a job, from doing stuff. Maybe some people let their kids stop them. An excuse, or whatever. But it ain't stopping me," she says firmly. "I had a maternity leave for three months from school. That was allowed. But I went back after a week. I wanted to.

"I think maybe I'll try for a job being an airline mechanic. The whole idea of working on those big things that fly around, that's cool. Plus, it's something that not everybody else is choosing, you know? Everybody picks nursing, or teaching, or stuff like that.

"I went to a college fair for school," she continues. "I wasn't looking for no colleges, but I was looking for airline mechanic stuff, you know? And I was talking to this one guy at his booth—a technician. He didn't know anything about it when he first started. But he joined the air force, and they taught him everything. Maybe that's what I'll do, join the air force. He was the first person I ever met that is what I want to be."

"Maybe I Think Too Much"

But now she is sixteen, and now she is nowhere near being able to join the air force. And, she says, her life is full of problems.

"Right now, my life is kind of falling apart," she says, her face void of emotion. "I get real depressed. I feel like I have to do so much for my mom; she depends on me too much. I handled her money, her bills. I had to go shopping for her. I can't do it no more. But she drinks and can't handle that stuff by herself.

"I help with my brothers and sisters. When I get my check, I sometimes have to get them clothes and shoes for school before I get stuff for me and Domanick. I mean, I don't mind sometimes. In a way, I feel like they are my family; I don't want them going without. She only gets six hundred dollars a month, and her rent is five hundred. I feel good when I help, but then I get mad because she isn't doing right by the kids. She drinks too much, spends too much time with Jaime.

"She's asked me to let my little sister Rachel come over here. Those young kids, ever since they came back out of the foster home, they act snotty. They don't want to do any work around the house, so she wants me to help discipline Rachel. But my mom, she comes around here and gets mad at me if I yell at Rachel. If I make her do dishes, my mom gets mad. My mom won't discipline her, but she acts all crazy when I do.

"I don't know," she says sadly. "Maybe I think too much. Lots of times I'll wake up real early in the morning and think about this stuff, and I can't go back to sleep, because it'll be on my mind. I think of the problems, the things I have to do.

"Plus, I think about Domanick, and I wish maybe I'd been older, like twenty-five, when I had him. I'm young. I was just getting to know my dad, and then he dies. It's all really hard."

Lisa says that sometimes she thinks back to when she was nine or ten and just getting to know her father.

"It was so weird," she says, "being out in California. He wouldn't let me smoke or drink. He acted like I was a little girl—called me 'baby,' stuff like that. Made me come in at a certain time, only let me have one cookie a day. He was so strict. I was drinking six-packs here, you know, but to him I was little, not old enough to stay out after dark. What would he think of me now, with a little kid of my own?"

Lisa exhales a long stream of smoke and looks out the window.

"I think about that sometimes."

Mary

> "I NEVER WORRIED ABOUT GETTING PREGNANT. I WASN'T ON BIRTH CONTROL, AND HE NEVER USED A CONDOM. I GUESS WE JUST FIGURED WE'D BE LUCKY."

She answers the door wrapped in a sheet, her eyes swollen from sleep. Her dark hair is tousled, and she is carrying a can of baby formula.

"I'm sorry, I didn't hear the bell," Mary says in a breathless voice. "I'm used to the baby waking me up, but she decided to sleep until . . . hey, what time *is* it, anyway?"

Mary peers into the kitchen at the clock.

"Wow!" she says, her face breaking into a big smile. "Ten-thirty!"

A Hard Way to Grow Up

She disappears into the basement and returns a moment later carrying a wide-eyed, redheaded baby.

"This is Cozette," Mary says proudly. "It means 'little pet.' I read it in that rock magazine, *Metal Edge*, you know? I heard the name and liked it right away; I knew I'd like to name a baby that.

"I'm eighteen, and I know that's young to be having babies," Mary says, more awake now. "But I really love having Cozette. She means the world to me . . . I can't tell you. I admit that I wasn't planning to have her yet, but I always knew I wanted a baby, ever since I was a little girl."

Being a little girl was a time not so far past, Mary knows. She has vivid memories of being small, and some of them are not happy ones.

"My parents fought a lot," she says. "My mom is profoundly deaf—that's how she's classified—and my father is deaf and mute. I'm not sure how they met each other, but they sure didn't get along. That was a hard way to grow up. I feel sorry for any kids whose parents fight that much, I'll tell you.

"Part of the trouble was my father's drinking," she says candidly. "He has always been a drinker. Even now, he is. In fact, when I go to see him, I have to tell him ahead of time when I'm coming over, so he stays sober. He's mean and he's violent, so we have to have someone there when we visit, just in case."

An especially vivid memory is when her father once tried to kill her mother with a knife—in front of his two small daughters.

"I think it started the way most of their fights started," says Mary. "He'd be drunk, and she didn't want him to be drunk. It may sound strange, a deaf-mute and a deaf person arguing and fighting, but they did. He could make plenty of noise, so you knew when he was mad. The only word he can say is *Paul*; that's the name of his friend. In fact, when my younger sister was born, my mom named her Paula, hoping that he could say her name.

"Anyway, this one time, he started fighting with her, pulled out a knife, and tried to kill her. My sister and I were there, just watching it happen. We were holding on to my mom's legs, just crying and screaming. He would have killed her for sure, but someone came and pulled him away. We went to a women's shelter after that."

SIGNING AT SIX MONTHS

Her mother's deafness?

"Not really a problem when we were growing up," she says. "I do know that when I was frightened by their fighting, I'd run off; my mom told me about that. She'd get panicky when she couldn't find me. I think her being hard of hearing made it easier for me to keep hidden!

"But usually it was fine, her being deaf. I learned to sign when I was real small. She taught me by signing to me as soon as we came home from the hospital. My first sign was at six months—bottle. My mom talks and signs; some people think she's hard to understand, but I'm used to it. I'm pretty good at it, although I tend to rely on finger spelling if I don't know the right sign."

Mary laughs, a sudden memory coming to mind.

"You know, when I was pretty little, like five or six, my mom wanted me to stay up late and sign a television show for her—*Knot's Landing*. I said, 'Mom, I have to go to school tomorrow; the show's on too late.' But she told me it would be okay. I should just tell my teacher that I was up late helping my mom."

MOVING AROUND

Her parents' marriage ended in divorce when Mary was five, and her mother soon remarried. That marriage lasted ten years.

"His name was Cliff, and he was deaf, too," says Mary. "I think they met at a club for deaf people. He and my mom had a daughter—my sister Callie. Her real name is Calista. Isn't that pretty?

"So anyway, we spent a lot of time moving around," she remembers. "Saint Cloud, Duluth, different parts of Minneapolis, South Dakota, Brainerd, Goodhue, Rochester . . . you name it, we've probably lived there.

"I'm not really sure why we left. I don't know if it had something to do with my father wanting custody of us, or just that my mom and Cliff weren't happy where they were living. It wasn't for employment, because neither of them worked."

Mary thinks about this and shakes her head.

"No, I guess that isn't completely right. Cliff worked sometimes. He'd get a job for a while as a cook, or doing outside work, or maybe in a factory or something. But nothing regular, you know what I mean?"

So much moving was difficult for a girl who was shy to begin with, Mary remembers ruefully.

"It wasn't just me it was hard on," she says. "My sister Paula had a hard time, too. We'd just get to a place, then we'd leave. It's funny how it just seemed so natural. I guess when you're a little kid, you just accept how your life is. We never really even asked.

"But we had lots of moves in the middle of a school year. Different friends, different teachers. I remember being in seventh grade, moving from Saint Cloud to Brooklyn Park. It was the middle of the year, right after Christmas, I think. Anyway, I kept getting lost in the new school. It made me so mad, because the school wasn't even as big as the school I'd just left back in Saint Cloud. It was just hard to find my way around. And of course you don't want to ask people, because then you look even more stupid.

"It was hard for me to talk to people, at least until high school," she says. "I had braces, and before my braces I was ashamed of my crooked teeth. So I just wouldn't talk to people, or I would talk without opening my mouth very wide. It wasn't a real good time for me, I guess."

A Disappointment

By the time she entered high school, Mary's orthodontic problems had been corrected, and she was less timid about talking to people. Even so, high school started out as a big disappointment for her.

"The kids bothered me, the way they acted," she says. "I'm not a racist person, but I felt like the black kids at my high school were treating me as though I were. Some of the black kids would shove the white kids around—especially the ninth graders—and

Mary's memories of childhood are the constant moves her parents put her through. Both she and her sister never felt as though they were able to make friends or have a stable life.

then get mad at us for not watching where we were going! I mean, they were the ones who ran into me, but they're yelling at me.

"That made me mad. And there was this one boy, a black kid, who yelled at me a lot. He embarrassed me, really. He said because I was white, I expected him to be his slave. That was not true! Anyway, it was always sort of uncomfortable and a little scary to go to school. And so one day, I just took off, just left. I did that almost every day for a while."

Finally, Mary says, she had a talk with her mother about it, and she asked if she could switch to a school that her friend attended and move in with her friend's family.

"It wasn't like I really wanted to leave home, or anything like that," says Mary. "I mean, I got along okay with my mom; we weren't fighting. But my mom was getting ready to move again, and I just didn't want to go through another move like that. She said it was okay, and that's what I did."

Having Boyfriends

Mary became sexually active at age fourteen, although, she says, it was definitely not her idea.

"I was forced into it," she maintains. "It was my best friend's boyfriend, and she knows about it. The boy kept bugging me, kept after me. My friend wasn't around. At first it seemed like he was just kidding, but after that it got scary. I didn't like that at all.

"The second time was better, because it was with a boy I really liked. I told my mom that I wanted to go on birth control. She wasn't happy about that, but there wasn't much she could do about it. She said, 'It's your life,' and she was right. She knew I was having a relationship and that it made sense for me to be protected.

"But the bad part was that we kept missing our appointment. See, because I was a minor, the clinic wanted my mom to come with me and give her okay. But we had things come up, so we just had to call and reschedule."

Mary looks down at Cozette and laughs, a good-natured chuckle.

"I guess we rescheduled once too often, huh?"

Her third boyfriend was Jamie, Cozette's father. She knew she was in love, she says, after going out with him two or three times.

"I was sixteen," Mary says, smiling. "I ran into him two times— once in line for Ozzy Osborne tickets and another time at a Poison concert. He's got great red hair and a great laugh. We started going out that summer, and I loved him right away.

"I never worried about getting pregnant," she says. "I wasn't on birth control, and he never used a condom. I guess we just figured we'd be lucky, so we didn't think about it too much. Besides, my friend Colleen had sex a lot more often than I did, and she'd never gotten pregnant."

A Sore Throat and a Pregnancy Test

She found out she was pregnant when she went to the emergency room about a bad sore throat.

Jamie holds his infant daughter. He and Mary became parents soon after they met and started dating.

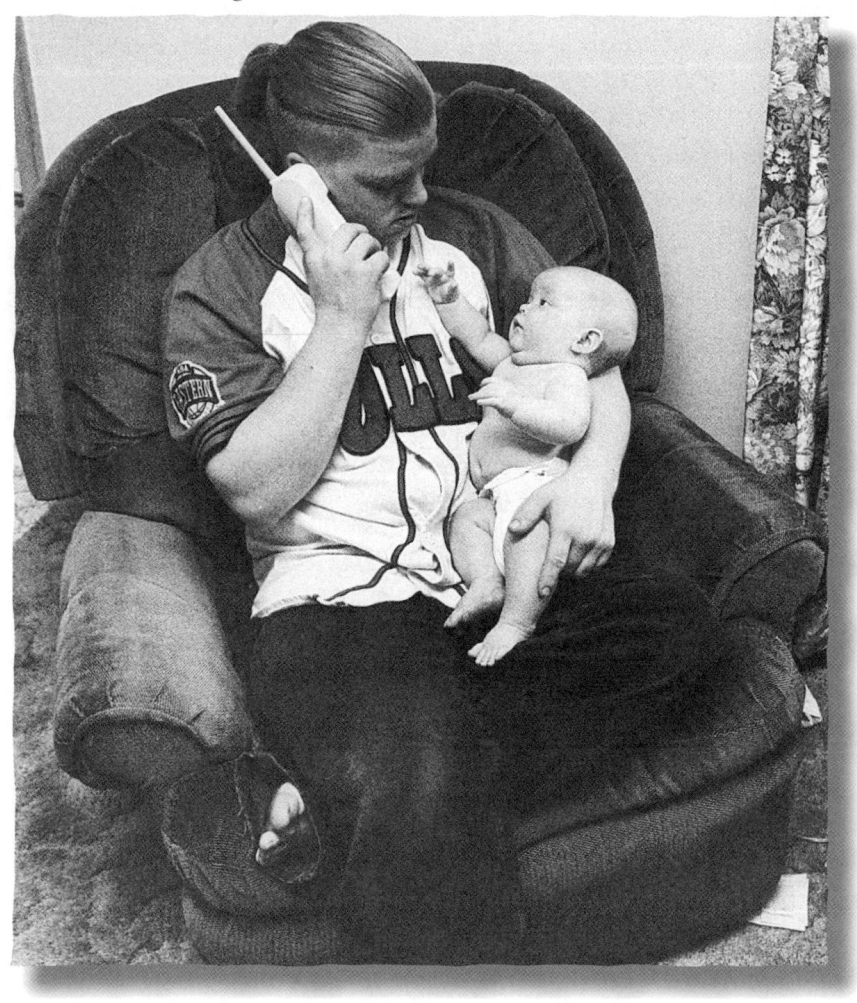

"I thought it was strep," she remembers. "I'm real susceptible, and I've ended up getting so sick from it that I have to go into the hospital. So I went in to the emergency room for a throat culture.

"Well, you know those routine questions they always make you fill out? Like, did you ever have surgery, or are you allergic to any medications? Well, the one question about when my last period was had me stumped. I thought for a while and decided it was August. And this was October when I was filling this out.

"The nurse saw that and asked me if I wanted to have a pregnancy test, and I figured I should."

Mary shrugs.

"I don't want to lie. I figured there was a good chance I was pregnant, since we'd been having sex without birth control. I didn't have any symptoms, though, and that made me think I might *not* be pregnant. Anyway, I waited for forty-five minutes while they did the test. I wasn't scared. I remember that much. Just really bored.

"I *did* get scared, though, when I saw the doctor come out and call my name. That really got to me, because I'd been watching him all that time. Usually when he came out with test results, he went over to the person in the waiting room and quietly talked to them. But here, with me, he was telling me to come into the examination room. I got really, really nervous."

The doctor confirmed what Mary suspected, that she was indeed pregnant.

"I had this funny look on my face, I guess," she says. "He said to me, 'This is not a planned pregnancy, is it?' And I said 'No.' I got really scared then, and my main plan was just not to cry while I was there in the hospital.

"I was really good, holding it in. I thought that if I could just make it until he stopped talking, I could get outside and cry all I wanted. Heck, I didn't even mind walking around downtown in tears, no matter who was around. It's hard to explain; I just didn't want those people in the hospital to see me cry."

TELLING PEOPLE

Mary confided in her friend Colleen right away, and her friend was shocked.

"She really was astonished," says Mary. "Like I said before, she always thought she'd get pregnant before I did, since she was lots more active than me. But I knew I had to tell her, since she'd been my best friend since eighth grade. I didn't want to tell Colleen's parents, though. I just didn't feel right telling them. It's funny, even though I was living with them, her father didn't find out until I was eight months along!"

Telling her own mother was a much scarier thought, says Mary.

"I wasn't going to tell her until I had to," she says. "She's thirty-seven, and I know she didn't want to be a grandma. That was one of the reasons she was dead set against me having sex so early. She always said, 'Don't make me a grandma before I'm forty.' But when I told her the next month, it was really strange. She was excited; she called everyone and told them about it!"

What about Jamie?

"I told him right after I told Colleen," says Mary. "I had broken up with him just the day before, too. I don't know exactly the reason—it wasn't a big fight or anything. It's just that we weren't spending enough time together. It was hard; I had school, and we both had jobs. The only time he was home was during the day. So schedules were really hard. I understood that. But he wasn't good about calling me, and I didn't like that. There were days that would go by when I didn't even hear from him, so I got fed up, I think.

"But I had to tell him, and I had a chance almost right away. He called to see what was going on, and he could tell I was in a bad mood. He asked me why, and I said, 'Because I'm pregnant, goddam it.'

"Boy," she remembers, "he was silent for the longest time. Finally he told me to come over and we'd talk about it. So that's what I did."

OPTIONS

Mary says that when she talked to Jamie, she brought up the idea of putting the baby up for adoption but that he rejected the idea.

"I knew abortion wasn't an option for me," she says firmly. "I didn't even consider it, because I don't believe in it. I'm not Catholic or anything, but it just seems wrong. I know too many people who have had an abortion and have really suffered afterwards. They think about it every day. That would have been me; I would have been bothered emotionally. I love babies, and I always knew I'd have a baby someday. I mean, I've been baby-sitting since I was nine years old—newborns and everything—so I love babies.

"Adoption was more like it, for me," she continues. "And even though Jamie thought I should keep the baby, I still kept thinking about it. And when I talked to my mom about it, she agreed with Jamie. She said, 'You know if you put that child up for adoption, someone in the family is going to adopt it.'

"See, that's happened three times in our family. We try to keep the kids in the family, the ones that aren't wanted by their natural parents, or whatever. Like my cousin got a girl pregnant, and she didn't want the baby, so my aunt and uncle adopted it.

"Anyway, I just kept thinking about it. I thought how I was really young and how I didn't want to be raising a child when I didn't have any money or anything. But when the baby kicked for the first time, and I felt that little kick, I stopped thinking about adoption. That was when I thought, there is no way that I could ever give this baby away."

"I'VE SEEN BAD PARENTING"

Mary says that even though she was unprepared for the pregnancy, she was certain that she could take good care of a baby.

"I knew that even though I might not have a lot of money or anything, I could be a real good mother," she says. "I've seen bad parenting, that's for sure. One time I baby-sat all day long; the mother was never home. There were four kids, from nine years old down to a tiny baby. But the mom would go out drinking, stay gone all day.

"Once when I was there, the older kids opened all the beer cans in the house and poured them down the sink. They said, 'That'll teach my mom and her friends.' I thought, boy. And I got yelled at, got blamed for it. But I really wasn't mad about what they did; I sort of agreed with them. Anyhow, those kids later got taken away from their mother, for neglect."

Even when a mother is not a drinker and her intentions are good, Mary knows, a child can have trouble. She remembers with a great deal of emotion how her mother had a mental breakdown when Mary was very small.

"Paula and I got put in foster homes because of that," says Mary. "I don't know where my dad was. My mom never talked about what happened with her, just that she was really sick. I

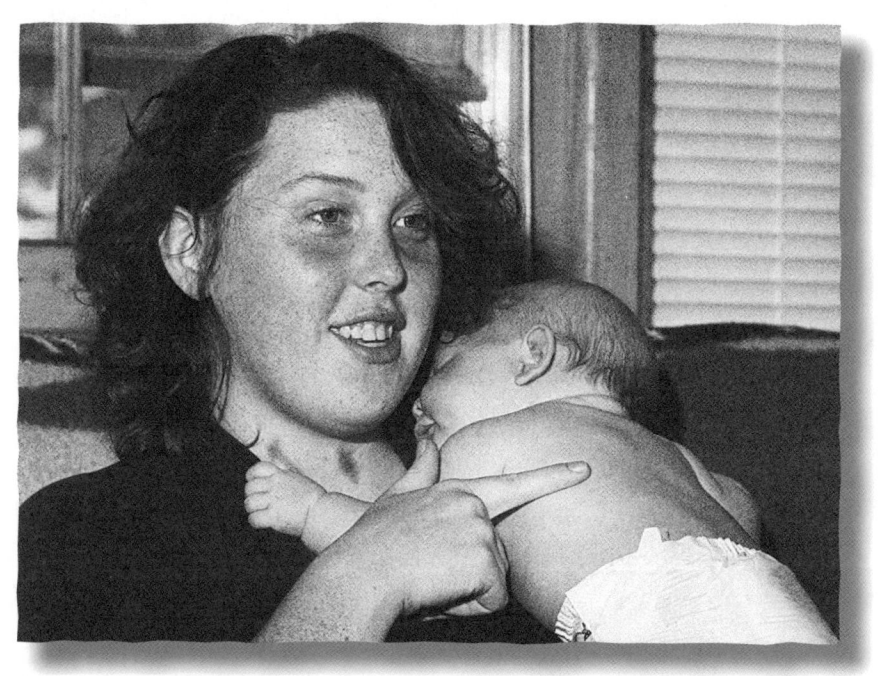

Mary decided to keep her baby rather than put it up for adoption: "When the baby kicked for the first time, and I felt that little kick, I stopped thinking about adoption. . . . There is no way that I could ever give this baby away."

remember that she was just standing there, holding my sister, just a really tiny baby. She was just standing there, shaking and shaking. A neighbor came over and my mom just dropped Paula. Luckily, the neighbor caught the baby before she hit the ground.

"That neighbor took Paula and me to her house, and they put my mom in a hospital. We stayed at the neighbor's for a while and then later went to a foster home."

Mary shudders.

"I still have nightmares about that," she says. "I had such a bad time there. I remember that I did something wrong; I'm not sure what. But I remember them dunking my head under water. Really, I still have dreams about that, about not being able to breathe. I'm not sure how long my sister and I were in the foster home, but I was so glad when we finally could go back home to my mom."

WAITING FOR THE BABY

Her pregnancy was easy, says Mary, and the time passed quickly.

"My friends are sort of mad at me," she smiles, "because I had like this textbook pregnancy. Never really sick, never in much discomfort. I'm a strong person; maybe that's the reason. Anyway, I did everything I did before, went to school right up until the day she was born.

"I *did* quit my job, though," she says, "but that had nothing to do with me being pregnant. Well, in a way it did, but not because I was sick or anything. See, I worked in Hardee's, and when my manager found out I was pregnant, she started really being mean. She gave me lectures, told me I had no goals in life, and that I was really no good.

"I never liked the job much anyway," she admits, "but that was a good reason to quit. I didn't need to be talked to that way. I always did my work. She had no reason to pick on me. Anyway, I quit that job and used my time after school to clean up my room so when the baby came everything would be ready."

Mary says that one thing did change during the last half of her pregnancy: she cut off her ties to Jamie.

"It's hard to explain," she says, laughing. "It's not that I stopped loving him or anything. But I just wanted to be left alone. I didn't like him bossing me around or telling me what to do. He had been getting on my nerves for a long time, ever since I was pregnant.

"Like he'd say, 'You better sign up for this program, or that program.' Stuff like that. Telling me what to do, when I already knew. I'm not stupid, and I didn't need that."

Mary measures her words carefully.

"You know, I was thinking about this, about why I didn't want him around? I think it was that I didn't want him in the labor room when the baby was born. I don't ever want a guy seeing that I might not be able to stand the pain. I'm one of these people that can take a lot; I'm strong. So I didn't want to have him there if I was screaming or if I had to ask for some painkillers, or whatever. I think that's the reason."

COZETTE AND HER FATHER

Because he and Mary were not talking, Jamie was not at the hospital when Cozette was born. He had no idea that Mary had had the baby, in fact.

"The birth was tiring—sixteen hours of hard labor," she says. "I had a friend there, and my mom was in and out. When the baby finally came out, I was so tired. I watched the nurses cleaning her up. I was glad to see her, and like I said, I knew right away what her name was.

"The hospital time went by in a rush. So many visitors . . . I got about ten minutes of sleep the whole time I was there. I thought a lot about Jamie, though. I wanted to let him know that his daughter was born."

Mary reached him soon after her release from the hospital. As it turned out, she says, Jamie had been calling quite a bit, but her friend Colleen had been screening her calls.

"She really made me mad," says Mary. "I mean, she was telling him I wasn't there, when I was. She'd get the phone and walk into the other room to talk, so I wouldn't know Jamie was on the line. All that time, I thought he just wasn't calling. But anyway, finally we talked, and he asked if he could see the baby.

"We made plans to meet the next day. I told him to meet us at the bus stop at 2:30. As our bus pulled up to his stop, I could see him out the window, just sitting there looking real nervous. I got off the bus, with Cozette in her car seat, and he took the car seat right out of my hands.

"He took the blanket off her, just a little, to peek at her. He just said two words: 'She's cute.' I knew he'd think that. I had a new outfit on her, pink and white, with little flowers. She looked great. I'll always remember that."

Mary says that Jamie started spending more time with them, although he was a little nervous around the baby.

"He always wanted to see her." she says. "But he didn't want to hold her, at least not right away. But after a while he figured she wasn't going to break, I guess. She cuddled up to him, and I could see that he liked that.

"Jamie is living with us here. It's just kind of a trial thing, to see if we can make a go of it. We decided to give it six months, to see if we can get along. So far . . . I don't know . . . it's okay, but no one knows what will happen, how things will turn out."

"SHE IS JUST MORE USED TO ME"

Mary says that her one complaint about Jamie is that he doesn't help much with Cozette.

"He spends most of his time doing what he likes to do, and that's play Nintendo," she says. "He really likes the football game that Nintendo has, NFL, or something like that. Jamie is good at football—real football—so I guess that's why. His class ring from high school has a little football on it and a number thirteen. That was his number when he played.

"Anyway, he plays a lot of Nintendo. I know he really loves me and Cozette, but I think he needs to be better at being helpful. I mean, when his friends come over, Jamie's personality changes a little bit. I get ignored. When his friends come over, I sit upstairs all day—me and Cozette. I mean, I'll be there for a little while, since some of his friends are my friends, too. But just for a while.

"My big gripe is that he won't take care of Cozette when other people are around," she says. "When it's just the three of us here, he'll take care of her—unless he's in the middle of a Nintendo

Although they became estranged before the baby was born, Jamie and Mary are trying to make a go of being together. "Jamie is living with us here. It's just kind of a trial thing. . . . We decided to give it six months, to see if we can get along."

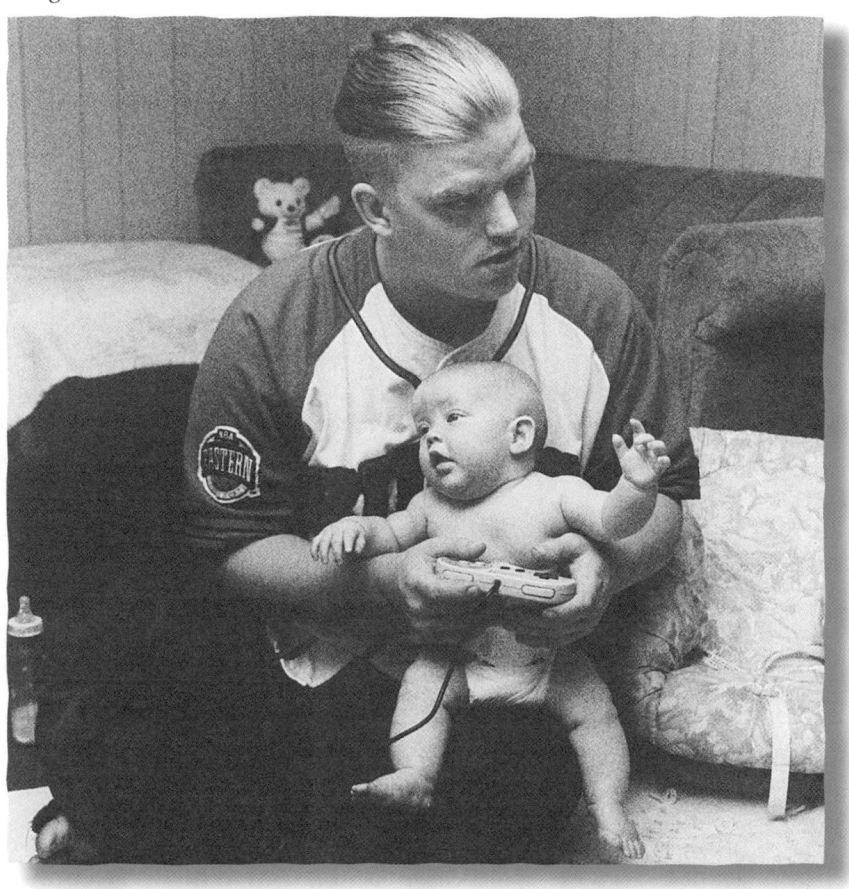

game, of course. And he tries to be a really good daddy. Like last night, she was just screaming. I don't know what the matter was. She was in her swing, and he took her out, got her a bottle.

"Well, she stopped crying for a while, then started again. No matter what he did, she went back to crying. I kept telling him, 'I'll take her, I'll take her.' But no, he said he would manage."

Mary laughs.

"I think the big thing with Jamie is that he wants to be able to do it, to make her stop crying. Once he finally handed her to me, she got quiet right away. And when she stopped crying like that, Jamie came down and said, 'You make me sick!' I think he was a little bit serious, you know? He sometimes says that Cozette hates him, but I told him that isn't true. She is just more used to me, that's all."

We're Just Trying to Figure Things Out

For now, Mary says, she and Jamie are just getting used to the idea of being parents, and of being partners.

"Jamie has finished school, so he's a little ahead of me," she says. "He's not working now, but he's trying to find something. He's got a line on a job at a shipping and loading company that would pay fourteen dollars an hour. That would be great. Right now we're living on his social security money that he gets for his knee. He was hit by a car when he was younger, and he has a bad knee.

"So we get that money, and I get money from WIC—that's Women, Infants, and Children. It's like a government program that gives money for formula and stuff. I get eight cans of formula free each month, and Cozette goes through it all. She's a hungry girl.

"I was receiving benefits because I'm a student, but they discontinued that. They said I never sent in a student report, but I did. See, I'm entitled to social security from my dad as long as I'm in school. I could sign up for AFDC, but I don't really want it. I don't like the idea of welfare. I want us to raise Cozette without depending on welfare, you know?"

Eventually, Mary says, she'd like to go to college and pursue a degree in medicine.

"I've always wanted to be a doctor, even when I was a little girl," she says. "I used to tell my mom that someday I'd be a doctor. Maybe I'll start out doing medical lab stuff, then work my way up. I am a good student when I put my mind to it."

"I Can Read for Hours and Not Get Bored"

Mary says that she has a head start on a lot of people in high school, since she likes to read so much, although she admits most of her favorite books aren't ones that will show up on a high school curriculum.

"I can read for hours and not get bored," she says, pulling out a handful of paperbacks from underneath the coffee table. "Look, there's tons of books, and they're all ones I've read. I like true-crime books the best—*Satan's Underground*, *Helter Skelter*. I don't get nightmares or anything from them, but some of them sure are gross.

"This one, *Lobster Boy*, was really something. There's one picture of Lobster Boy with four bullet holes in his head. It didn't gross me out or anything. But all I could think of was, boy, that must have hurt.

"And another one I read was even more creepy. It was the story of a little girl whose parents were in a satanic cult. They forced her to eat cut-up eyes and penises and everything of her friends when she was really little. That was something."

She reads a lot to Cozette, too, although those are much different kinds of books.

"She has books all over the place, too," says Mary. "She likes the sound of my voice, and we read all the time. I want her to be a good reader when she's older. That's important to me. Jeez, when I think about it, I was reading to her before she was even born. It seems funny, maybe, but I think it was good for her."

I'm a Daughter, Too

Although most of her energy and time is taken up with her infant daughter, Mary says that her mother is still an important part of her life—and a part that needs special attention now.

"My mom has been having trouble recently, and I've got to remember that besides being somebody's mother, I'm still somebody's daughter, and somebody's big sister," she says. "Although my sister Paula is living with a friend's family, Mom has her hands full right now, with my little sister Callie. She's six, and she's just like I was, my mom tells me, a real tomboy. She gets mad at my mom and hits her. She's not only wild like that, but she's a spitter, too. She's pretty accurate, too. My mom has threatened to put her in a foster home if she doesn't change her ways.

"It's hard for Callie, I know. When I was like that, my mom would send me to my room. But I think my mom doesn't have the patience with Callie that she had with us older ones. One thing mom does is she has this system of using stuffed animals.

"The way it works is this: we were supposed to have one stuffed animal that we used to signal to my mom that we were hurting, that we felt bad. I had a bear; Paula had a little gorilla. Callie has one, too. Anyway, whenever my mom gets mad at her, Callie's supposed to get the animal out and hug it. My mom says she doesn't want to hurt her any more than she's been hurt, you know? It's like a reminder to her to back off. Mom just gets frustrated and needs that reminder sometimes."

SHE'S GOT PROBLEMS RIGHT NOW

Mary says that her mother has had difficulty with a landlord recently and is trying to find a new place to live.

"She's in an emergency shelter right now," says Mary. "She and Callie are there; I guess they have till the end of the month to stay there. I haven't got a car, so I haven't been into the city to visit, but the place sounds okay.

"The problem was this: the caretaker didn't like my mom. He broke into her apartment and picked up Callie and was going to slap her. That caretaker is a racist; he doesn't like my mom because she has a couple of friends who are black and who visited her there.

"Anyway, she doesn't want to live there, and she's saving up for another place to live. She needs to get a deposit together. It's hard for my mom, because at the shelter she doesn't have access to the stuff she had before—the phone with a light that flashes, stuff like that. See, she doesn't hear the phone and hardly ever can hear someone knocking at the door. If Callie's not in the room with her, she'd never even hear the fire alarm if it went off.

"So, sometimes Callie calls me and wants to 'talk' to Cozette. She needs a lot of attention right now, and I try to do that. But then, I think I should be spending more time trying to get this relationship figured out with Jamie. I get worried sometimes that I'm not doing enough for anybody."

Right Now

Mary says that she really has no social life; that would be almost impossible with a baby so young. However, one thing that saddens her is that the birth of her daughter has driven a wedge between her and her best friend. Instead of being happy for her, Mary says, Colleen acts as though she has been betrayed.

"I think she's jealous of the baby," says Mary sadly. "Or maybe it's my relationship with Jamie. She's upset that we're living here, that I'm not staying with her and her family any more. She told me, 'You have no time for me; you have the baby.'

"Well, I told her that I could still talk, hang out a little bit," says Mary. "Just because I have a baby and a boyfriend doesn't mean I don't need a friend, you know? But I don't think she gets it.

"Yesterday she told me she'd gone out to Lakeville. She knows I'd like to have gone. She said, 'We would have invited you, *but . . .*' and she looked right at Cozette."

Mary seems to be a mother to more than Cozette: Her younger sister needs her help, her mother asks her advice, and her boyfriend seems to also rely on her for guidance.

Mary shakes her head.

"I hope she gets over it. I told her that she's the baby's godmother, but the way she's acting, I don't know. Anyway, my social life is pretty much nonexistent. One of Jamie's friends has a girlfriend who's due pretty soon. Sometimes she comes over, and while the guys are downstairs playing Nintendo, we talk. She asks me lots of questions about what the delivery was like, stuff like that.

"And I'm trying to get along with Jamie. He's even trying to teach me to play one of his video games——Mortal Kombat. That one's not so bad, I guess; I mean, the football game is so boring to me. But anyway, he's trying to teach me to play. He's like, 'Come on, Mary, this is this guy's move.' I try, anyway. I don't get how to make the little guys jump. I can punch and hurl those fireballs, but I haven't figured out jumping yet. Maybe in about five years. . . ."

Mary looks down at the baby in her lap.

"Oh, wow, I just thought of something. In five years I'll be getting Cozette ready to start kindergarten. Buying new school shoes or something. That's hard to imagine. But it's something important to think about, anyway."

She picks up Cozette and looks closely into her eyes and smiles. Cozette grins and squeals, excited by the attention.

"You're going to be the prettiest little redheaded girl in the class, aren't you?" Mary laughs.

Epilogue

Since the four teenage mothers in this book were interviewed, a number of changes have taken place, which readers will no doubt find interesting.

Kay is working part-time at a temp agency. She works the night shift, and Jasmine spends that time at her grandmother's house. She is still seeing Tano, although she maintains that it is not a permanent relationship.

Mary has had to put her schoolwork on hold for a time. Her mother suffered a severe asthma attack and has been hospitalized, and Mary has been taking care of her little sister Callie. Jamie found a part-time job, and little Cozette is growing quickly.

Safa is happy that she is in her last trimester of high school. She has applications for three colleges, and is excited about the prospects ahead. Mahari's father is still in jail on the murder charge. Her mother and Frank are going to be married soon, she says, although she has cut off all ties with her mother. She prefers not to discuss that part of her life for now, she says.

Lisa is pregnant again. Dan is back in school up north, and is happy about the baby. Lisa says she is happy too, but she knows it will be even harder with two small children.

Ways You Can Get Involved

The Alan Guttmacher Institute
111 Fifth Ave.
New York, NY 10003
Works to develop family planning programs through research and public education.

Children's Defense Fund
25 E St. NW
Washington, DC 20001
Promotes the interests of all children, but especially the poor, minorities, or handicapped.

Planned Parenthood
810 Seventh Ave.
New York, NY 10019
Provides counseling about contraceptives and services through clinics around the United States.

Project Reality
P.O. Box 97
Golf, IL 60029
Encouraging abstinence as the best pregnancy preventative, this organization has developed an educational curriculum for junior and senior high schools.

Sex Information and Education Council of the U.S. (SIECUS)
130 W. 42nd St., Suite 2500
New York, NY 10036
One of the largest clearinghouses for information about pregnancy and related issues.

For Further Reading

Judy Berlfein, *Teen Pregnancy.* San Diego: Lucent Books, 1992. A good overview of the issues related to teen pregnancy, punctuated with many first-person interviews.

Leon Dash, *When Children Want Children: The Urban Crisis of Teenage Childbearing.* New York: William Morrow and Company, 1989. Challenging reading, but well documented.

Joy G. Dryfoos, *Putting Boys in the Picture: A Review of Programs to Promote Sexual Responsibility Among Young Males.* Santa Cruz, CA: Network Publications, 1988. A good source, helpful in understanding teen pregnancy from the father's point of view.

David Elkind, *All Grown Up and No Place to Go.* Reading, MA: Addison Wesley Publishing Company, 1984. Well-researched, interesting reading.

Nancy J. Kolodny, Robert C. Kolodny, and Thomas E. Bratter, *Smart Choices.* Boston, MA: Little, Brown and Company, 1986. Helpful bibliography.

Jeanne Warren Lindsay, *Teens Parenting: The Challenge of Babies and Toddlers.* Buena Park, CA: Morning Glory Press, 1981. Well illustrated and easy reading.

Paula McGuire, *It Won't Happen to Me: Teenagers Talk About Pregnancy.* New York: Dell, 1983. Very readable, with good emphasis on options for pregnant teens.

Laura Schlessinger, *Ten Stupid Things Women Do to Mess Up Their Lives.* New York: Bantam Books, 1995. A good section on "stupid pregnancy" gives a realistic portrayal of why pregnancy will not solve a young person's needs for love and affection.

Karin Swisher, ed., *Teenage Sexuality: Opposing Viewpoints.* San Diego, CA: Greenhaven Press, 1994. Presents a variety of viewpoints about teenage sexuality; excellent index.

Index

abortion
    as option for teen mothers, 15
    rejected by Mary, 80
    rejected by Safa, 37
adoption
    rejected by Kay, 17-18
    rejected by Mary, 81
alcohol
    teens and, 54-55
alcoholism, 31-33

Clinton, Bill, 8

Dan (boyfriend of Lisa)
    attitude toward graduating high school, 64
    gang experiences of, 60-63
    other child of, 63-64
drug addiction, 33-34
drugs
    in poor neighborhoods, 44-45

education
    options for teen mothers, 18

Gingrich, Newt, 8

Jaime (boyfriend of Mary)
    attitude toward baby, 84-86

Kay
    attitude toward infant daughter, 20
    birth experience of, 18-19
    boredom with lack of social life, 26
    childhood of, 11
    dropped out of high school, 18
    economic situation of, 20-21
    experience at abortion clinic, 15
    government support of, 23-24
    reaction of parents to pregnancy, 15-17
    reaction to learning about pregnancy, 14-15
    regrets about motherhood, 10
    relationship with Tony, 20
    resentment of parents, 24-25
    role of baby's father, 22-23
    sexual abuse of, 11-13
    telling mother about, 15
    thoughts on preventing daughter's pregnancy, 28

Lisa
    abuse of by mother's boyfriend, 55
    attitudes toward
        birth control, 56-57
        pregnancy, 57
        raising child, 65-66
        school, 70-71
    childhood of, 51-53
    competition with mom, 67-69
    foster care experience of, 59-60
    goals of, 71
    in juvenile center, 59
    introduction to alcohol by mother, 54
    meeting with father, 52-53
    poor mother of, 53-54
    poor neighborhood of, 50-51
    reaction of mother to pregnancy, 58
    reaction to birth of son, 60
    welfare and, 66

Mahari (son of Safa), 29

Mary
- attitudes on
  - abortion, 80
  - adoption, 81
  - baby's dad, 86
  - birth control, 77-78
  - daughter, 73
- birth experience of, 83
- childhood of, 74-76
- divorce of parents, 75
- early sexual activity of, 77
- love of reading, 87
- mother of
  - instability of, 82
- reaction of
  - friends to pregnancy, 79-80
  - friends toward baby, 89-90
  - parents to pregnancy, 80
  - to pregnancy, 79
- responsibility for mother, 88

poverty
- teen pregnancies and, 6

pregnancy
- teen myths about, 7

Project Solo, 23-24

racism, 45

Safa
- attitudes on
  - completing high school, 46
  - motherhood, 48
  - racism, 45
- childhood of, 31
- early sexual activity of, 34-35
- economic pressures of, 41-42
- how she discovered pregnancy, 35
- lack of bonding with parents, 41
- maturation of, 44
- mother of
  - crack addiction, 33
- reaction of
  - baby's father to pregnancy, 38
  - mother to pregnancy, 37
  - to son's birth, 39
- regrets about motherhood, 48-49
- relationship with mother, 31-32
  - after baby's birth, 40
- thoughts on being independent, 30

sex education, 71

sexual abuse
- role in early sexual activity, 12-13

sexual activity
- early, 34
- sexual abuse as cause of, 12-13
- teen, 6

teen dad
- lack of support of baby, 42
- reaction to pregnancy, 14-15, 38

teen mothers
- bleak statistics of, 7

teen pregnancies
- number of, 6

teens
- desire to have a baby and, 7

Tony (father of Kay's baby), 19
- Kay's opinion of, 26-28
- mother of
  - role in caring for Kay's baby, 21-22

welfare
- number of teen mothers on, 8

About the Author

Gail B. Stewart is the author of more than eighty books for children and young adults. She lives in Minneapolis, Minnesota, with her husband Carl and their sons Ted, Eliot, and Flynn. When she is not writing, she spends her time reading, walking, and watching her sons play soccer.

Although she has enjoyed working on each of her books, she says that *The Other America* series has been especially gratifying. "So many of my past books have involved extensive research," she says, "but most of it has been library work—journals, magazines, books. But for these books, the main research has been very human. Spending the day with a little girl who has AIDS, or having lunch in a soup kitchen with a homeless man—these kinds of things give you insight that a library alone just can't match."

Stewart hopes that readers of this series will experience some of the same insights—perhaps even being motivated to use some of the suggestions at the end of each book to become involved with someone of the Other America.

About the Photographer

Mark Ahlstrom has worked in publishing for over twenty years, producing over two hundred books for young adults.